The DHAMMAPADA

The MOTHER

LOTUS
PRESS

Twin Lakes, WI
U.S.A.

This book is copyright under the Berne Convention. Apart from any fair dealing for the purpose of private study, research, criticism or review, as permitted under the Copyright Act, 1956, no portion may be reproduced by any process without written permission. Enquiries should be addressed to the publisher.

© Sri Aurobindo Ashram 2004

First U.S. Edition 2004
Published by Lotus Press by arrangement with Sri Aurobindo Ashram, Copyright Department, Pondicherry, India 605002.

Lotus Press, P.O. Box 325, Twin Lakes, Wisconsin 53181.
Web: www.lotuspress.com   Email: lotuspress@lotuspress.com
(800) 824-6396

ISBN: 0-940985-25-X

Library of Congress Control Number: 2004097351

Printed in the United States of America.

Contents

Conjugate Verses

Every Friday I shall read out to you a few verses of the Dhamma-pada, then we shall meditate on that text. This is to teach you mental control. If I think it necessary I shall give you an explanation.

The Dhammapada begins with conjugate verses; here is the first one:

> *In all things the primordial element is mind. Mind pre-dominates. Everything proceeds from mind.*

Naturally, this concerns the physical life, there is no question of the universe.

> *If a man speaks or acts with an evil mind, suffering follows him as the wheel follows the hoof of the bullock that pulls the cart.*

That is to say, ordinary human life, such as it is in the present world, is ruled by the mind; therefore the most important thing is to control one's mind; so we shall follow a graded or "conjugate" discipline, to use the Dhammapada's expression, in order to develop and control our minds.

There are four movements which are usually consecutive, but which in the end may be simultaneous: to observe one's thoughts is the first, to watch over one's thoughts is the second, to control one's thoughts is the third and to master one's thoughts is the fourth. To observe, to watch over, to control, to master. All that to get rid of an evil mind, for we are told that the man who acts or speaks with an evil mind is followed by suffering as closely as the wheel follows the hoof of a bullock that ploughs or draws the cart.

3

This is our first meditation.

30 August 1957

Mind predominates. Everything proceeds from mind. In all things the primordial element is mind. If a man speaks or acts with a purified mind, happiness accompanies him as closely as his inseparable shadow.

This is the counterpart of what we read last time. The Dhammapada contrasts a purified mind with an evil mind. We have already said that there are four successive stages for the purification of the mind. A purified mind is naturally a mind that does not admit any wrong thought, and we have seen that the complete mastery of thought which is required to gain this result is the last achievement in the four stages I have spoken of. The first is: to observe one's mind.

Do not believe that it is such an easy thing, for to observe your thoughts, you must first of all separate yourself from them. In the ordinary state, the ordinary man does not distinguish himself from his thoughts. He does not even know that he thinks. He thinks by habit. And if he is asked all of a sudden, "What are you thinking of?", he knows nothing about it. That is to say, ninety-five times out of a hundred he will answer, "I do not know." There is a complete identification between the movement of thought and the consciousness of the being.

To observe the thought, the first movement then is to step back and look at it, to separate yourself from your thoughts so that the movement of the consciousness and that of thought may not be confused. Thus when we say that one must observe one's thoughts, do not believe that it is so simple; it is the first step. I suggest that this evening in our meditation we take up this first exercise which consists in standing back from one's thought and looking at it.

6 September 1957

"He has insulted me, he has beaten me, he has humiliated me, he has robbed me." Those who nourish thoughts such as these never appease their hatred.

The Dhammapada tells us first of all that bad thoughts bring about suffering and good thoughts bring about happiness. Now it gives examples of what bad thoughts are and tells us how to avoid suffering. Here is the first example, I repeat: "He has insulted me, he has beaten me, he has humiliated me, he has robbed me"; and it adds: "Those who nourish thoughts such as these never appease their hatred."

We have begun our mental discipline, basing ourselves on the successive stages of mental development and we have seen that this discipline consists of four consecutive movements, which we have described in this way, as you surely remember: to observe, to watch over, to control and to master; and in the course of the last lesson we have learnt — I hope — to separate ourselves from our thoughts so as to be able to observe them as an attentive spectator.

Today we have to learn how to watch over these thoughts. First you look at them and then you watch over them. Learn to look at them as an enlightened judge so that you may distinguish between the good and the bad, between thoughts that are useful and those that are harmful, between constructive thoughts that lead to victory and defeatist thoughts which turn us away from it. It is this power of discernment that we must acquire now; that will be the subject of our meditation tonight.

As I have told you, the Dhammapada will give us examples, but examples are only examples. We must ourselves learn how to distinguish thoughts that are good from those that are not, and for that you must observe, as I have said, like an enlightened judge — that is to say, as impartially as possible; it is one of the most indispensable conditions.

13 September 1957

5

*"He has insulted me, he has beaten me, he has humili-
ated me, he has robbed me." Those who do not nourish
thoughts such as these foster no hatred.*

This is the counterpart of what we read the other day. But
note that this concerns only thoughts that generate resentment.
It is because rancour, along with jealousy, is one of the most
widespread causes of human misery.

But how to avoid having rancour? A large and generous
heart is certainly the best means, but that is not within the reach
of all. Controlling one's thought may be of more general use.

Thought-control is the third step of our mental discipline.
Once the enlightened judge of our consciousness has distin-
guished between useful and harmful thoughts, the inner guard
will come and allow to pass only approved thoughts, strictly
refusing admission to all undesirable elements.

With a commanding gesture the guard will refuse entry to
every bad thought and push it back as far as possible.

It is this movement of admission and refusal that we call
thought-control and this will be the subject of our meditation
tonight.

20 September 1957

*For, in truth, in this world hatred is not appeased by
hatred; hatred is appeased by love alone. This is the
eternal law.*

This is one of the most celebrated verses of the Dhammapada,
one of those most often cited — I would have liked to be able to
say, "one of the most obeyed in the world"; unfortunately that
would not be true. For people speak much of this teaching but
do not follow it.

Yet, there is one aspect of the problem which is less spoken
of but which seems perhaps more urgent still if you want things
to change in the world, something to which people give very little

thought. I am going to surprise you. It is this: if love must be returned for hatred in order that the world may change, would it not be even more natural that love should be returned for Love?

If one considers the life and action and heart of men as they are, one would have every right to be surprised at all the hatred, contempt, or at best, the indifference which are returned for this immensity of Love which the divine Grace pours upon the world, for this immensity of Love which acts upon the world at every second to lead it towards the divine delight and which finds so poor a response in the human heart. But people have compassion only for the wicked, the deficient, the misshapen, for the unsuccessful ones and the failures — truly it is an encouragement to wickedness and failure.

If one thought a little more of this aspect of the problem, perhaps one would have less need to insist on the necessity of returning love for hatred, because if the human heart responded in all sincerity to the Love that is being poured into it with the spontaneous gratitude of a love which understands and appreciates, then things would change quickly in the world.

27 September 1957

Many are those who are not aware that one day we all must die. And those who are aware of it appease their quarrels.

When you think you may die the next moment, immediately, automatically, there occurs in you a detachment from all material things; it is logical that from then on you think only of what does not depend upon this physical life and which is the only thing that will still belong to you once you have left this body, that is to say, the eternal existence. The Buddha did not use the word "Divine", but it is essentially the same thing.

To think that one might die the next moment was formerly, in the ancient initiations, a discipline that one had to follow for a certain time, for the reason I have just mentioned and also in order to overcome all fear of death and to accustom oneself to it. In that age and at the time when the Dhammapada was spoken by the Buddha, the possibility of an earthly immortality was never mentioned because this possibility belonged to such a far-off future that there would have been no point in speaking of it.

Today Sri Aurobindo tells us that this possibility is near at hand and that we have only to prepare for it. But the essential condition even to prepare for it is to completely abolish all fear of death.

You must neither fear it nor desire it.

Stand above it, in an absolute tranquillity, neither fear it nor desire it.

4 October 1957

Just as the strong wind uproots a feeble tree, so Mara overwhelms the man who lives only in pursuit of pleasure, who does not control his senses, who knows not how to moderate his appetite, who is lazy and wastes his energies.

In Buddhist literature, Mara represents the Spirit of Evil, all that is contrary or opposed to the spiritual life; in certain cases he represents death — not so much physical death as death to truth, to the spiritual being.

Here, it means that so long as one does not control one's senses and desires, and concerns oneself with external material satisfactions as the most important thing, one has not the will necessary to resist the attack of hostile forces and all that pulls us down and leads us away from the spiritual reality.

The Dhammapada does not take its stand so much on the moral point of view; it is not evil as men understand it with their blind justice and their arbitrary sense of good and bad. Evil, from the spiritual point of view, is truly that which leads us away from the goal, which sometimes even tears us away from the deepest purpose of our existence, from the truth of our being and prevents us from realising it.

This is the way in which it should be understood.

11 October 1957

Just as the strong wind has no hold upon a mighty rock, so Mara has no hold upon a man who does not live in pursuit of pleasure, who has good control of his senses, who knows how to moderate his appetite, who is endowed with unshakable faith and who wastes not his energies.

What the Dhammapada means when it speaks of faith is not at all the belief in a dogma or a religion, it is not even faith in the teaching of the Master; it is faith in one's own possibilities, the certitude that whatever the difficulties, whatever the obstacles, whatever the imperfections, even the negations in the being, one is born for the realisation and one *will* realise.

The will must never falter, the effort must be persevering and the faith unshakable. Then instead of spending years to realise what one has to realise, one can do it in a few months, sometimes even in a few days and, if there is sufficient intensity, in a few hours. That is to say, you can take a position within yourself and no bad will that attacks the realisation will have any more power over you than the storm has over a rock.

After that, the way is no longer difficult; it becomes extraordinarily interesting.

18 October 1957

He who puts on the yellow robe while he is yet impure, lacking in self-control and lacking in loyalty, truly he is unworthy to wear the yellow robe of the monk.

Of course, the yellow robe, in the literal sense, is the robe of the Buddhist monks; it became the robe of all who practised asceticism. But this is not what the Dhammapada truly means to say, because there is no lack of men who wear the yellow robe but are not purified of their taints. The yellow robe is taken as the symbol of consecration to the spiritual life, the external sign of renunciation of all that is not an exclusive concentration upon the spiritual life.

What Buddhism means by "impurities" is chiefly egoism and ignorance; because, from the Buddhist standpoint, the greatest of all taints is ignorance, not ignorance of external things, of the laws of Nature and of all that you learn at school, but the ignorance of the deepest truth of things, of the law of the being, of the Dharma.

It is noteworthy that the two defects insisted upon here are lack of self-control and lack of loyalty. Loyalty means here sincerity, honesty; what the Dhammapada censures most severely is hypocrisy: to pretend that you want to live the spiritual life and not to do it, to pretend that you want to seek the truth and not to do it, to display the external signs of consecration to the divine life — here symbolised by the yellow robe — but within to be concerned only with oneself, one's selfishness and one's own needs.

It is interesting to note the insistence of the Dhammapada on self-control, for according to the Buddhist teaching, excess in all things is bad. The Buddha always insisted on the Middle Path. You must not be too much on one side nor too much on the other, exaggerate one thing or the other. You must have measure, balance in all things, the balance of moderation.

Therefore the qualities that make you worthy of leading the spiritual life are to have an inner balance, a balance in your action, and to be moderate in everything, to be sincere, honest, loyal.

Balance, moderation, loyalty, honesty: this is the subject of our meditation.

8 November 1957

But he who has discarded all impurity, who is firmly attached to the precepts of morality, who knows how to moderate his appetite and who is loyal, he, truly, is worthy to wear the yellow robe.

I would not like you to take this text as a moral catechism. It certainly has a much deeper and truer meaning, because in all truly spiritual teachings, morality as it is mentally conceived is out of place.

So too the word "impurity". Pure, as it is understood morally, has not at all the meaning it is given in a truly spiritual teaching; and particularly from the Buddhist standpoint, purity is absence of ignorance, as I have already told you last time, and ignorance means ignoring the inner law, the truth of the being. And loyalty means not to take the illusion for the reality, the changing and fluctuating appearances for the inner and real permanence of the being.

We can say then that self-control and self-mastery, measure, absence of desire, the search for the inner truth of the being and the law of its self-manifestation are very necessary preoccupations for those who want to practise the spiritual life.

To be true to oneself, to one's goal, not to let oneself be moved by disorderly impulses, not to take the changing appearances for the Reality, these are the virtues that one must have in order to progress on the way of spirituality.

15 November 1957

Those who take error for truth, and the truth for error, will never attain the supreme goal, for they are led astray by vain desires and false views.

A comment could be added; for, if one were satisfied with taking error for truth and truth for error, it should be logically very easy to make one's choice as soon as one found for some reason or other or with some help, what is truly the truth and what is

11

truly the error; one adopts the truth and rejects the error. But unfortunately one loves one's error, somewhere in the being there is an unwillingness to recognise what is true.

My experience is like this: whenever you sincerely want to know the truth, you do know it. There is *always* something to point out the error to you, to make you recognise the truth. And if you observe yourself attentively you find out that it is because you prefer error that you do not find the truth.

Even in small details, the very smallest — not to speak of the big things of life, the big decisions that one has to take — even in the smallest things, whenever the aspiration for the truth and the will to be true are wholly sincere, the indication always comes. And precisely, with the method of the Buddhist discipline, if you follow up within yourself the causes of your way of being, you always find out that persistence in error comes from desire. It is because you have the preference, the desire to feel, to act, to think in a particular way, that you make the mistake. It is not simply because you do not know what is true. You do not know it precisely because you say in a vague, general, imprecise way, "Oh, I want the truth." In fact, if you take a detail, each detail, and put your finger on it, you discover that you are playing the ostrich in order not to see. You put up something uncertain, something vague, a veil, in order not to see behind it.

Whenever there is sincerity, you find that the help, the guidance, the grace are always there to give you the answer and you are not mistaken for long.

It is this sincerity in the aspiration for progress, in the will for truth, in the need to be truly pure — pure as it is understood in the spiritual life — it is this sincerity which is the key to all progress. With it you know — and you *can*.

There is always, somewhere in the being, something which prefers to deceive itself, otherwise the light is there, always ready to guide, but you shut your eyes in order not to see it.

22 November 1957

12

Those who know the true to be true and the false to be false, they attain the supreme goal, for they pursue right desires and correct views.

We saw last time that it is not sufficient to be able to distinguish what is right from what is wrong. At first sight this seems to be the most difficult point. It is quite obvious that if everyone had to find it out for himself, it would be a very long work; you can pass your whole life going through innumerable experiences which little by little will enlighten you as to what is right and what is not.

Therefore it is easier to rely on someone who has done the work before you and whom you have simply to ask, "Is this true? Is that false?" Evidently, that offers a great advantage, but unfortunately it is not always sufficient; for if you have the desire that things should be in a certain way and that what you prefer should be right, then you are not always ready to listen to good advice.

The last sentence, "for they pursue right desires", which seems to be a commonplace, is perhaps the most difficult part of the problem.

In this book, in this teaching, there are short sentences that appear so simple. If you read without sufficient reflection, you tell yourself, "But it is self-evident, you recognise as true what is true and as false what is false, what does that mean then?" But first of all it is not so easy to distinguish what is true from what is not, then to recognise, that is to say, to admit that a certain thing is true; and above all it is more difficult still perhaps to recognise that a certain thing is false.

In reality, in order to discern exactly what is false requires such sincerity in the aspiration, such resolution in the will to be true that even this little phrase "to know the true to be true and the false to be false" means a very considerable realisation. And the conclusion, "they attain the supreme goal" is a great promise.

There are teachings which say that one must have no desire at all; they are the ones that aim at a complete withdrawal from life in order to enter into the immobility of the Spirit, the absence of all activity, all movement, all form, all external reality. To attain that one must have no desire at all, that is to say, one must completely leave behind all will for progress; progress itself becomes something unreal and external. But if in your conception of Yoga you keep the idea of progress, and if you admit that the whole universe follows a progression, then what you have to do is to shift the objective of desire; instead of turning it towards things that are external, artificial, superficial and egoistical, you must join it as a force of realisation to the aspiration directed to the truth.

These few words, "they pursue right desires", are a proof that the teaching of the Buddha, in its essence, did not turn away from the realisation upon earth, but only from what is false in the conception of the world and in activities as they are carried on in the world. Thus when he teaches that one must escape from life, it is not to escape from a life that would be the expression of the truth but from the illusory life as it is ordinarily lived in the world.

Sri Aurobindo tells us that in order to reach the Truth and to have the power of realising this Truth you must join the spiritual consciousness to a progressive mental consciousness.

And these few words certainly prove that such was the original conception of the Buddhist teaching.

6 December 1957

Just as the rain penetrates through the thatch of a leaking roof, so the passions penetrate an unbalanced mind.

There are innumerable small Buddhist sects of all kinds, in China, in Japan, in Burma, and each one follows its own methods; but the most widespread among them are those whose sole practice is to make the mind quiet.

They sit down for a few hours in the day and even at night and quiet their mind. This is for them the key to all realisation — a quiet mind that knows how to keep quiet for hours together without roving. You must not believe however that it is a very easy thing to do, but they have no other object. They do not concentrate upon any thought, they do not try to understand better, to know more, nothing of the kind; for them the only way is to have a quiet mind and sometimes they pass through years and years of effort before they arrive at this result — to silence the mind, to keep it absolutely silent and still; for, as it is said here in the Dhammapada, if the mind is unbalanced, then this constant movement of ideas following one another, sometimes without any order, ideas contradicting and opposing each other, ideas that speculate on things, all that jostles about in the head, makes holes in the roof, as it were. So through these holes all undesirable movements enter into the consciousness, as water enters into a house with a leaky roof.

However that may be, I believe it is a practice to be recommended to everyone: to keep a certain time every day for trying to make the mind quiet, even, still. And it is an undeniable fact that the more mentally developed one is, the quicker one succeeds; and the more the mind is in a rudimentary state, the more difficult it is.

Those who are at the bottom of the scale, who have never trained their minds, find it necessary to speak in order to think. It happens even that it is the sound of their voice which enables them to associate ideas; if they do not express them, they do not think. At a higher level there are those who still have to move words about in their heads in order to think, even though they do not utter them aloud. Those who truly begin to think are those who are able to think without words, that is to say, to be in contact with the idea and express it through a wide variety of words and phrases. There are higher degrees — many higher degrees — but those who think without words truly begin to reach an intellectual state and for them it is much easier to make

15

the mind quiet, that is to say, to stop the movement of associating the words that constantly move about like passers-by in a public square, and to contemplate an idea in silence.

I emphasise this fact because there are quite a few people who, when mental silence has been transmitted to them by occult means, are immediately alarmed and afraid of losing their intelligence. Because they can no longer think, they fear they may become stupid! But to cease thinking is a much higher achievement than to be able to spin out thoughts endlessly and it demands a much greater development.

So from every point of view, and not only from the spiritual point of view, it is always very good to practise silence for a few minutes, at least twice a day, but it must be a true silence, not merely abstention from talking.

Now let us try to be completely silent for a few minutes.

(*Meditation*)

13 December 1957

Just as the rain cannot penetrate a house well covered with thatch, so also the passions cannot penetrate a balanced mind.

(*It begins to rain.*) That's it. The mind of the sky must be out of balance. (*Laughter*) It is raining.

So I think the sky has no balance and it is better for you to go home. (*It rains harder.*) Well, there is nothing to be done!

The balance is not being restored. You should all go home and meditate on the necessity of having a balanced mind. That's all.

20 December 1957

In the two worlds, in this world and in the other, one who does evil grieves. He laments and suffers as he recalls his evil deeds.

16

It is quite evident that when you act in an ugly and mean way, naturally you are unhappy; but to be unhappy because you are conscious of the ugliness of your actions seems to me to be already a very advanced stage, for one needs to be very conscious in order to be aware of the evil that one does, and to be conscious of the evil that one does is already a first step towards not doing it any more.

Generally, people are altogether blind to the ugliness of their own actions. They do wrong through ignorance, through unconsciousness, through smallness, through that sort of doubling back on oneself which comes from unconsciousness and ignorance, that obscure instinct of self-preservation which makes one ready to sacrifice the whole world for the sake of one's own well-being. And the smaller one is, the more natural appears the sacrifice offered to one's smallness.

One must be very much higher on the scale to see that what one does is ugly. One must already have at the core of oneself a kind of foreknowledge of what beauty, nobility, generosity are, to be able to suffer from the fact that one doesn't carry them within oneself.

I think the Dhammapada speaks here of those who already know what is beautiful and noble and who do evil wilfully, deliberately. For them life becomes terribly painful indeed. To do persistently what one knows should not be done, is at the cost of all peace, all possible tranquillity, all the well-being that one can have. He who lies is constantly uneasy in the fear that his lie may be discovered; he who has acted wrongly is in a constant anxiety at the idea that perhaps he will be punished; he who tries to deceive has no peace lest it should be found out that he deceives.

In reality, even for a purely egoistic reason, to do good, to be just, straight, honest is the best means to be quiet and peaceful, to reduce one's anxiety to a minimum. And if, besides, one could be disinterested, free from personal motives and egoism, then it would be possible to become truly happy.

You carry with you, around you, in you, the atmosphere created by your actions, and if what you do is beautiful, good and harmonious, your atmosphere is beautiful, good and harmonious; on the other hand, if you live in a sordid selfishness, unscrupulous self-interest, ruthless bad will, that is what you will breathe every moment of your life and that means misery, constant uneasiness; it means ugliness that despairs of its own ugliness.

And you must not believe that by leaving the body you will free yourself of this atmosphere; on the contrary, the body is a kind of a veil of unconsciousness which diminishes the intensity of the suffering. If you are without the protection of the body in the most material vital life, the suffering becomes much more acute and you no longer have the opportunity to change what is to be changed, to correct what is to be corrected, to open yourself to a higher, happier and more luminous life and consciousness.

You must make haste to do your work here, for it is here that you can truly do it.

Expect nothing from death. Life is your salvation.

It is in life that you must transform yourself. It is upon earth that you progress and it is upon earth that you realise. It is in the body that you win the Victory.

27 December 1957

One who does good rejoices in the two worlds, in this world and in the other. He rejoices more and more as he recalls his good deeds.

One who does evil suffers in the two worlds, in this world and in the other. "I have done wrong": this thought torments him. And his torments increase still more as he follows the way which leads to the infernal world.

One who does good rejoices in the two worlds, in this

world and in the other. "I have done good": the thought
rejoices him and his happiness increases more and more
as he follows the way that leads to the celestial world.

It would almost seem from these texts that Buddhism accepts
the idea of a hell and a heaven; but that is quite a superficial way
of understanding; for, in a deeper sense, this was not the thought
of the Buddha. The idea on which he always insisted is that you
create, by your conduct and the state of your consciousness, the
world in which you live. Everyone carries in himself the world
in which he lives and in which he will continue to live even when
he loses his body, because, according to the Buddha's teaching,
there is, so to say, no difference between life in the body and life
outside the body.

Some persons believe, some traditions teach that to leave the
body is a blessing and that all difficulties disappear, provided,
however, you fulfil certain rites, as in some religions, and that is
also why so much importance is given to the religious rites which
are, as it were, a passport for going to a happier region once you
have left the body. Some even imagine that as soon as you leave
the body you at once leave your miseries behind; but it is far
from being true and this is what the Dhammapada points out
here: what it calls the infernal world consists of psychological
ranges, particular states of consciousness you enter when you
do wrong, that is to say, when you stray away from all that is
beautiful, pure, happy and you live in ugliness and wickedness.
Nothing is more disheartening than to live in an atmosphere of
wickedness.

What the Dhammapada says here in an almost puerile way
is essentially true. Naturally, it does not refer to those who think,
"Oh, how good I am, how nice I am!" and therefore feel happy.
That is childishness. But when you are good, when you are
generous, noble, disinterested, kind, you create in you, around
you, a particular atmosphere and this atmosphere is a sort of
luminous release. You breathe, you blossom like a flower in

19

the sun; there is no painful recoil on yourself, no bitterness, no revolt, no miseries. Spontaneously, naturally, the atmosphere becomes luminous and the air you breathe is full of happiness. And this is the air that you breathe, in your body and out of your body, in the waking state and in the state of sleep, in life and in the passage beyond life, outside earthly life until your new life.

Every wrong action produces on the consciousness the effect of a wind that withers, of a cold that freezes or of burning flames that consume.

Every good and kind deed brings light, restfulness, joy — the sunshine in which flowers bloom.

3 January 1958

Even though he may recite a great number of sacred texts, if he does not act accordingly, the foolish one will be like the cowherd who counts the cows of others. He cannot share in the life of the disciples of the Blessed One.

Though he may recite only a tiny portion of the sacred texts, if he puts into practice their teaching, having rejected all passion, all ill-will and all delusion, he possesses the true wisdom; his mind completely freed, no longer attached to anything, belonging neither to this world nor to any other, he shares in the life of the disciples of the Blessed One.

The thing has been so often said and repeated that it seems quite unnecessary to insist on the fact that a mite of practice is infinitely more precious than mountains of talk. Surely, all the energy that one spends in explaining a theory would be much better utilised in overcoming in oneself a weakness or a defect.

Therefore to conform to the wisdom of this teaching, we

20

shall consider the best means of rejecting all passion and ill-will and delusion.

The delusion consists in taking the appearance for the reality and transient things for the only thing worthy of pursuit, the everlasting Truth.

It is rather interesting to note that the Dhammapada clearly underlines that it is not enough to be free from the bonds of this world only, but of all the worlds.

For the true and zealous Buddhists tell you that ordinary religions captivate you by enticing you with the glittering advantages that you will find after death in their Paradise, if you practise their principles. Buddhism, on the other hand, has neither hell nor heaven. It does not terrify you with eternal punishment nor does it tempt you with celestial felicities.

It is in the pure Truth that you will find your satisfaction and the reward of all your efforts.

10 January 1958

Vigilance

Vigilance is the way that leads to immortality (or Nirvana). Negligence is the way that leads to death. Those who are vigilant do not die. Those who are negligent are dead already.

In these texts the word Nirvana is not used in the sense of annihilation, as you see, but in the sense of an eternal existence in opposition to life and death, as we know them in the present earthly existence, and which are contrary to each other: life contrary to death, death contrary to life. It is not *that* life which is spoken of, but the eternal existence which is beyond life and death — the true existence.

Vigilance means to be awake, to be on one's guard, to be sincere — never to be taken by surprise. When you want to do sadhana, at each moment of your life, there is a choice between taking a step that leads to the goal and falling asleep or sometimes even going backwards, telling yourself, "Oh, later on, not immediately" — sitting down on the way.

To be vigilant is not merely to resist what pulls you downward, but above all to be alert in order not to lose any opportunity to progress, any opportunity to overcome a weakness, to resist a temptation, any opportunity to learn something, to correct something, to master something. If you are vigilant, you can do in a few days what would otherwise take years. If you are vigilant, you change each circumstance of your life, each action, each movement into an occasion for coming nearer the goal.

There are two kinds of vigilance, active and passive. There is a vigilance that gives you a warning if you are about to make a mistake, if you are making a wrong choice, if you are being weak or allowing yourself to be tempted, and there is the active vigilance which seeks an opportunity to progress, seeks to utilise every circumstance to advance more quickly.

There is a difference between preventing yourself from falling and advancing more quickly.

And both are absolutely necessary.

He who is not vigilant is already dead. He has lost contact with the true purpose of existence and of life.

So the hours, circumstances, life pass in vain, bringing nothing, and you awake from your somnolence in a hole from which it is very difficult to escape.

17 January 1958

Having fully understood what vigilance is, the sages delight in it and take their pleasure in the presence of the Great Ones.

Throughout this teaching there is one thing to be noticed; it is this: you are never told that to live well, to think well, is the result of a struggle or of a sacrifice; on the contrary it is a delightful state which cures all suffering. At that time, the time of the Buddha, to live a spiritual life was a joy, a beatitude, the happiest state, which freed you from all the troubles of the world, all the sufferings, all the cares, making you happy, satisfied, contented.

It is the materialism of modern times that has turned spiritual effort into a hard struggle and a sacrifice, a painful renunciation of all the so-called joys of life.

This insistence on the exclusive reality of the physical world, of physical pleasures, physical joys, physical possessions, is the result of the whole materialistic tendency of human civilisation. It was unthinkable in ancient times. On the contrary, withdrawal, concentration, liberation from all material cares, consecration to the spiritual joy, that was happiness indeed.

From this point of view it is quite evident that humanity is far from having progressed; and those who were born into the world in the centres of materialistic civilisation have in their subconscient this horrible notion that only material realities are real and that to be concerned with things that are not material represents a wonderful spirit of sacrifice, an almost sublime effort. Not to be preoccupied from dawn to dusk and from dusk to dawn with all the little physical satisfactions, physical pleasures, physical sensations, physical preoccupations, is to bear evidence of a remarkable spirit. One is not aware of it, but the whole of modern civilisation is built on this conception: "Ah, what you can touch, you are sure that is true; what you can see, you are sure that is true; what you have eaten, you are sure of having eaten it; but all the rest — pooh! We are not sure whether they are not vain dreams and whether we are not giving up the real for the unreal, the substance for the shadow. After all, what are you going to gain? A few dreams! But when you have some coins in your pocket, you are sure that they are there!"

And that is everywhere, underneath everything. Scratch the appearances just a little, it is there, within your consciousness; and from time to time you hear this thing whispering within you, "Take care, don't be taken in." Indeed, it is lamentable.

We have been told that evolution is progressive and that it follows a spiral of ascending progression. I do not doubt that what one calls comfort in modern cities is a much higher degree of evolution than the comfort of the cave-man. But in ancient narratives, they always spoke of a power of foresight, of the prophetic spirit, the announcement of future events through visions, life's intimacy with something more subtle that had for the simple people of that age a more concrete reality.

Now, in those beautiful cities that are so comfortable, when one wants to condemn anything, what does one say? — "It's a dream, it is imagination."

And precisely, if a person lives in an inner perception, people look at him slightly askance and wonder whether he is altogether mentally sound. One who does not pass his time in striving for wealth or in trying to increase his comforts and well-being, to secure a good position and become an important person, a man who is not like that is mistrusted, people wonder whether he is in his right mind.

And all that is so much the stuff of the atmosphere, the content of the air you breathe, the orientation of the thoughts received from others that it seems absolutely natural. You do not feel that it is a grotesque monstrosity.

To become a little more conscious of oneself, to enter into relation with the life behind the appearances, does not seem to you to be the greatest good. When you sit in a comfortable chair, in front of a lavish meal, when you fill your stomach with delicious dishes, that certainly appears to you much more concrete and much more interesting. And if you look at the day that has passed, if you take stock of your day, if you have had some material advantage, some pleasure, a physical satisfaction, you mark it as a good day; but if you have received a good lesson from life, if it has given you a knock on your nose to tell you that you are a stupid fellow, you do not give thanks to the Grace, you say, "Oh, life is not always fun!"

When I read these ancient texts, I really have the impression that from the inner point of view, from the point of view of the true life, we have fallen back terribly and that for the acquisition of a few ingenious mechanisms, a few encouragements to physical laziness, the acquisition of instruments and gadgets that lessen the effort of living, we have renounced the reality of the inner life. It is that sense which has been lost and it needs an effort for you to think of learning the meaning of life, the purpose of existence, the goal towards which we must advance, towards which all life advances, whether you want it or not. One step towards the goal, oh! it needs so much effort to do that. And generally one thinks of it only when the outer circumstances are not pleasant.

How far we are from the times when the shepherd, who did not go to school and kept watch over his flock at night under the stars, could read in the stars what was going to happen, commune with something which expressed itself through Nature, and had the sense of the profound beauty and that peace which a simple life gives!

It is very unfortunate that one has to give up one thing in order to gain another. When I speak of the inner life, I am far from opposing any modern inventions, far from it, but how much these inventions have made us artificial and stupid! How much we have lost the sense of true beauty, how much we burden ourselves with useless needs!

Perhaps the time has come to continue the ascent in the curve of the spiral and now with all that this knowledge of matter has brought us, we shall be able to give to our spiritual progress a more solid basis. Strong with what we have learnt of the secrets of material Nature, we shall be able to join the two extremes and rediscover the supreme Reality in the very heart of the atom.

24 January 1958

Those who are intelligent, meditative, persevering, who ceaselessly struggle with themselves, attain to Nirvana, which is the supreme felicity.

Whosoever can sustain his zeal, remain pure in his actions, act wisely, restrain his passions, live according to the Law (or to morality), he shall see his renown increase.

This promise of a good name does not seem to me quite worthy of the Buddhist teaching. It probably meant something else. And to live according to morality, one must know which morality is intended, for if it is the usually recognised social morality, that also does not seem to me a very alluring promise. Those who have decided to abandon all worldly weaknesses certainly do not care about satisfying social morality... nor about acquiring a good name!

26

To sustain one's zeal is an excellent thing, to remain pure in one's actions is also indispensable, to act wisely is also perfect, one cannot do it too often; to restrain one's passions, that goes without saying, is the beginning... but that conclusion!!

However I see "Dhamma" has been translated here as "Law", and "Yasa" as "renown", whereas Dhamma should mean rather the inner truth and Yasa the spiritual glory. So we can interpret the text in this way: "Whosoever can sustain his zeal, remain pure in his actions, act wisely, restrain his passions, live according to the inner truth, he shall see his spiritual glory ever growing."

Thus understood, this text is quite excellent. One cannot do better than to conform to it.

31 January 1958 and 7 February 1958

By his effort, his vigilance, his discipline and self-mastery, the intelligent man should create for himself an island which no flood can submerge.

The fools, devoid of intelligence, give themselves up to negligence. The true sage guards vigilance as his most precious treasure.

Do not let yourself fall into carelessness, nor into the pleasures of the senses. He who is vigilant and given to meditation acquires a great happiness.

The intelligent man who by his vigilance has dispelled negligence, mounts to the heights of wisdom, whence he looks upon the many afflicted as one on a mountain looks down upon the people of the plain.

Vigilant among those who are negligent, perfectly awake among those who sleep, the intelligent man advances like a rapid steed leaving behind a weary horse.

Vigilance is admired. Negligence is reproved. By vigilance, Indra became the highest among the gods.

The Bhikkhu[1] who delights in vigilance and who shuns negligence advances like a fire consuming all bonds, both small and great.

The Bhikkhu who takes pleasure in vigilance and who shuns negligence can no longer fall. He draws near to Nirvana.

I have read out to you the whole chapter because it seemed to me that it is the totality of the verses that creates an atmosphere and that they are meant to be taken all together and not each one separately. But I strongly recommend to you not to take the words used here in their usual literal sense.

Thus, for example, I am quite convinced that the original thought did not mean that you are to be vigilant in order that you may be admired and that you must not be negligent in order not to be reproved. Besides, the example given proves it, for certainly it was not for the sake of gaining admiration that Indra, the chief of the overmental gods in the Hindu tradition, practised vigilance. It is a very childish way of saying things. Yet, if you take these verses all together, they have by their repetition and insistence, a power that evokes the thing which seeks expression; it puts you in relation with a psychological attitude which is very useful and has a very considerable effect, if you follow this discipline.

The last two verses particularly are very evocative. The Bhikkhu moves forward like a burning flame of aspiration and he shuns negligence.

Negligence truly means the relaxation of the will which makes one forget his goal and pass his time in doing all kinds

---

[1] Member of the Sangha (Buddhist community), mendicant monk who owns nothing.

of things which, far from contributing towards the goal to be attained, stop you on the path and often turn you away from it. Therefore the flame of aspiration makes the Bhikkhu shun negligence. Every moment he remembers that time is relatively short, that one must not waste it on the way, one must go quickly, as quickly as possible, without losing a moment. And one who is vigilant, who does not waste his time, sees his bonds falling, every one, great and small; all his difficulties vanish, because of his vigilance; and if he persists in his attitude, finding in it entire satisfaction, it happens after a time that the happiness he feels in being vigilant becomes so strong that he would soon feel very unhappy if he were to lose this vigilance.

It is a fact that when one has made an effort not to lose time on the way, any time lost becomes a suffering and one can find no pleasure of any kind in it. And once you are in that state, once this effort for progress and transformation becomes the most important thing in your life, the thing to which you give constant thought, then indeed you are on the way towards the eternal existence, the truth of your being.

Certainly there is a moment in the course of the inner growth when far from having to make an effort to concentrate, to become absorbed in the contemplation and the seeking of the truth and its best expression — what the Buddhists call meditation — you feel, on the contrary, a kind of relief, ease, rest, joy, and to have to come out of that in order to deal with things that are not essential, everything that may seem like a waste of time, becomes terribly painful. External activities get reduced to what is absolutely necessary, to those that are done as service to the Divine. All that is futile, useless, precisely those things which seem like a waste of time and effort, all that, far from giving the least satisfaction, creates a kind of discomfort and fatigue; you feel happy only when you are concentrated on your goal.

Then you are really on the way.

14 February 1958

The Mind

Just as the arrow-maker straightens his arrows, so also the intelligent man straightens his thoughts, wavering and fickle, difficult to keep straight, difficult to master.

Just as a fish cast out of the water, our mind quivers and gasps when it leaves behind the kingdom of Mara.

Difficult to master and unstable is the mind, forever in search of pleasure. It is good to govern it. A mind that is controlled brings happiness.

The sage should remain master of his thoughts, for they are subtle and difficult to seize and always in search of pleasure. A mind that is well guided brings happiness.

Wandering afar, solitary, bodiless and hidden in the deep cave of the heart, such is the mind. Whosoever succeeds in bringing it under control liberates himself from the fetters of Mara.

The intelligence of one whose mind is unstable, who is ignorant of the true Law, and whose faith is wavering will never be able to develop.

If a man's thoughts are not agitated, if his mind is not troubled by desire, if he no longer cares for good and evil, this man, wide awake, knows nothing of fear.

Observing that the body is as fragile as a jar, and fortifying the mind like a city at arms, one should attack Mara with the blade of intelligence and should guard carefully whatever has been won.

Before long this body will be lying on the earth, abandoned, as lifeless as a piece of old wood.

Whatever an enemy may do to an enemy, whatever a hater may do to a hater, the harm caused by a misdirected mind is even greater still.

Neither mother nor father nor any other kinsman can do so much good as a well-directed mind.

These few verses correspond to all the needs of those whose mind has not been mastered. They point out the attachment that one has to one's old ways of being, thinking and reacting, even when one is trying to get away from them. As soon as you emerge by your effort, you are like a fish out of water and you gasp for breath because you are no longer in your element of obscure desires.

Even when you make a resolution, the mind remains unstable. It is subtle, difficult to seize. Without seeming to do so, it is continually seeking its own satisfaction; and its intentions are hidden in the core of the heart so as not to show their true nature.

And while not forgetting the weakness of the body, you must try to strengthen the mind against its own weakness; with the sword of wisdom, you must fight against the hostile forces and treasure the progress you have made so that these forces may not despoil you of your progress, for they are terrible thieves.

And then there is a short couplet for those who are afraid of death, intended to liberate them from that fear. Finally there is a last short couplet for those who are attached to their family to show them the vanity of this attachment.

In the end, a last warning: an ill-directed, ill-controlled thought does more harm than an enemy can do to an enemy or a hater to a hater. That is to say, even those who have the best intentions in the world, if they do not have a wise control over their thought, will do more harm to themselves and to those whom they love than an enemy can do to an enemy or a hater to a hater.

The mind has a power of deception in its own regard which is incalculable. It clothes its desires and preferences with all kinds of wonderful intentions and it hides its trickeries, resentments and disappointments under the most favourable appearances.

To overcome all that, you must have the fearlessness of a true warrior, and an honesty, a straightforwardness, a sincerity that never fail.

28 February 1958

The Flowers

Who will conquer this world of illusion and the kingdom of Yama[1] and the world of the gods? Who will discover the path of the Law as the skilled gardener discovers the rarest of flowers?

The disciple on the right path will conquer this world of illusion and the kingdom of Yama and the world of the gods. He will discover the path of the Law as the skilled gardener discovers the rarest of flowers.

Knowing his body to be as impermanent as foam and as illusory as a mirage, the disciple on the right path will shatter the flowery arrow of Mara and will rise beyond the reach of the King of Death.

Death carries away the man who seeks only the flowers of sensual pleasure just as torrential floods carry away a sleeping village.

Death, the destroyer, overcomes the man who seeks only the flowers of sensual pleasure before he can satisfy himself.

The sage should go from door to door in his village, as the bee gathers honey from the flowers without bringing harm to their colours or their fragrance.

Do not criticise others for what they do or have not done, but be aware of what, yourself, you do or have not done.

---

[1] The God of Death.

Just as a beautiful flower which is radiant yet lacks fragrance, so are the beautiful words of one who does not act accordingly.

Just as a beautiful flower which is both radiant and sweetly scented, so are the beautiful words of one who acts accordingly.

Just as many garlands can be made from a heap of flowers, so a mortal can accumulate much merit by good deeds.

The fragrance of flowers, even that of sandalwood or of incense, even that of jasmine, cannot go against the wind; but the sweet fragrance of intelligence goes against the wind. All around the man of intelligence spreads the fragrance of his virtue.

No fragrance, not even that of sandalwood or incense, nor of the lotus nor of jasmine, can be compared with the fragrance of intelligence.

Weak is the fragrance of incense or sandalwood compared to that of a virtuous man which reaches up to the highest of divinities.

Mara cannot discover the way that those beings follow who lead a life of perfect purity and who are liberated by their total knowledge.

As the beautiful scented lily rises by the wayside, even so the disciple of the Perfectly Enlightened One,[2] radiant with intelligence, rises from the blind and ignorant multitude.

---

[2] The Buddha.

There are some very wise recommendations here, for example, not to concern oneself with what others do nor with the mistakes they make, but to attend to one's own faults and negligences and rectify them. Another wise counsel is never to utter too many eloquent words which are not effectuated in action — speak little, act well. Beautiful words, they say, that are mere words, are like flowers without fragrance.

And finally, lest you get discouraged by your own faults, the Dhammapada gives you this solacing image: the purest lily can spring out of a heap of rubbish by the wayside. That is to say, there is nothing so rotten that it cannot give birth to the purest realisation.

Whatever may be the past, whatever may be the faults committed, whatever the ignorance in which one might have lived, one carries deep within oneself the supreme purity which can translate itself into a wonderful realisation.

The whole point is to think of that, to concentrate on that and not to be concerned with all the difficulties and obstacles and hindrances.

Concentrate exclusively on what you want to be, forget as entirely as possible what you do not want to be.

7 March 1958

The Fool

Long is the night for one who sleeps not; long is the road for one who is weary; long is the cycle of births for the fool who knows not the true law.

If a man cannot find a companion who is his superior or even his equal, he should resolutely follow a solitary path; for no good can come from companionship with a fool.

The fool torments himself by thinking, "This son is mine, this wealth is mine." How can he possess sons and riches, who does not possess himself?

The fool who recognises his foolishness is at least wise in that. But the fool who thinks he is intelligent, is a fool indeed.

Even if the fool serves an intelligent man throughout his life, he will nevertheless remain ignorant of the truth, just as the spoon knows not the taste of the soup.

If an intelligent man serves a wise man, if only for a moment, he will quickly understand the truth, just as the tongue instantly perceives the savour of the soup.

The fools, those who are ignorant, have no worse enemies than themselves; bitter is the fruit they gather from their evil actions.

The evil action which one repents later brings only regrets and the fruit one reaps will be tears and lamentations.

The good action one does not need to repent later brings no regret and the fruit one reaps will be contentment and satisfaction.

As long as the evil action has not borne its fruits, the fool imagines that it is as sweet as honey. But when this action bears its fruits, he reaps only suffering.

Though month after month the fool takes his food with the tip of a blade of Kusa grass,[1] he is not for all that worth a sixteenth part of one who has understood the truth.

An evil action does not yield its fruits immediately, just as milk does not at once turn sour; but like a fire covered with ashes, even so smoulders the evil action.

Whatever vain knowledge a fool may have been able to acquire, it leads him only to his ruin, for it breaks his head and destroys his worthier nature.

The foolish monk thirsts after reputation, and a high rank among the Bhikkhus, after authority in the monastery and veneration from ordinary men.

"Let ordinary men and holy ones esteem highly what I have done; let them obey me!" This is the longing of the fool, whose pride increases more and more.

One path leads to earthly gain and quite another leads to Nirvana. Knowing this, the Bhikkhu, the disciple of the Perfectly Enlightened One, longs no more for honour, but rather cultivates solitude.

---

[1] Kusa grass is considered sacred in India. Taking one's food with the tip of a blade of Kusa grass symbolises an act of asceticism.

This seems to point directly to hypocrites who take up the external forms and appearances of wisdom but in their hearts keep all the desires, ambitions, the need for show, and live to satisfy this ambition and these desires instead of living for the only thing that is worth living for: attainment of the true consciousness, integral self-giving to the Divine, the peace, the light and the delight that come from the true wisdom and self-forgetfulness.

One could easily replace throughout this text the word fool by the word ego. One who lives in his ego, for his ego, in the hope of satisfying his ego is a fool. Unless you transcend ego, unless you reach a state of consciousness in which ego has no reason for existing, you cannot hope to attain the goal.

The ego seems to have been indispensable at one time for the formation of the individual consciousness, but with the ego were born all the obstacles, sufferings, difficulties, all that now appears to us as adverse and anti-divine forces. But these forces themselves were a necessity for attaining an inner purification and the liberation from ego. The ego is at once the result of their action and the cause of their prolongation. When the ego disappears, the adverse forces will also disappear, having no longer any reason for their existence in the world.

With the inner liberation, with a total sincerity and perfect purity, all suffering will disappear, because it will no longer be necessary for the progress of the consciousness towards its final goal.

Wisdom, then, consists in working energetically at the inner transformation so that you may emerge victorious from a struggle which will have borne its fruits but will no longer have any need to exist.

14 March 1958

The Sage

We should seek the company of the sage who shows us our faults, as if he were showing us a hidden treasure; it is best to cultivate relations with such a man because he cannot be harmful to us. He will bring us only good.

One who exhorts us to good and dissuades us from doing evil is appreciated, esteemed by the just man and hated by the unjust.

Do not seek the company or friendship of men of base character, but let us consort with men of worth and let us seek friendship with the best among men.

He who drinks directly from the source of the Teaching lives happy in serenity of mind. The sage delights always in the Teaching imparted by the noble disciples of the Buddha.

Those who build waterways lead the water where they want; those who make arrows straighten them; carpenters shape their wood; the sage controls himself.

No more than a mighty rock can be shaken by the wind, can the sage be moved by praise or blame.

The sage who has steeped himself in the Teaching, becomes perfectly peaceful like a deep lake, calm and clear.

Wherever he may be, the true sage renounces all pleasures. Neither sorrow nor happiness can move him.

Neither for his own sake, nor for the sake of others does the sage desire children, riches or domains. He does not aim for his own success by unjust ways. Such a man is virtuous, wise and just.

Few men cross to the other shore. Most men remain and do no more than run up and down along this shore.

But those who live according to the Teaching cross beyond the realm of Death, however difficult may be the passage.

The sage will leave behind the dark ways of existence, but he will follow the way of light. He will leave his home for the homeless life and in solitude will seek the joy which is so difficult to find.

Having renounced all desires and attachments of the senses, the sage will cleanse himself of all the taints of the mind.

One whose mind is well established in all the degrees of knowledge, who, detached from all things, delights in his renunciation, and who has mastered his appetites, he is resplendent, and even in this world he attains Nirvana.

There is a sentence here which is particularly felicitous. It is the very first sentence we have read, "We should seek the company of the sage who shows our faults, as if he were showing us a hidden treasure."

In all Scriptures meant to help mankind to progress, it is always said that you must be very grateful to those who show you your faults and so you must seek their company; but the form used here is particularly felicitous: if a fault is shown to you it is as if a treasure were shown to you; that is to say, each time that you discover in yourself a fault, incapacity, lack of understanding, weakness, insincerity, all that prevents you from making a progress, it is as if you discovered a wonderful treasure.

Instead of growing sad and telling yourself, "Oh, there is still another defect", you should, on the contrary, rejoice as if you had made a wonderful acquisition, because you have just caught hold of one of those things that prevented you from progressing. And once you have caught hold of it, pull it out! For those who practise a yogic discipline consider that the moment you know that a thing should not be, you have the power to remove it, discard it, destroy it.

To discover a fault is an acquisition. It is as though a flood of light had come to replace the little speck of obscurity which has just been driven out.

When you follow a yogic discipline, you must not accept this weakness, this baseness, this lack of will, which means that knowledge is not immediately followed by power. To know that a thing should not be and yet continue to allow it to be is such a sign of weakness that it is not accepted in any serious discipline, it is a lack of will that verges on insincerity. You know that a thing should not be and the moment you know it, you are the one who decides that it shall not be. For knowledge and power are essentially the same thing — that is to say, you must not admit in any part of your being this shadow of bad will which is in contradiction to the central will for progress and which makes you impotent, without courage, without strength in the face of an evil that you must destroy.

To sin through ignorance is not a sin; that is part of the general evil in the world as it is, but to sin when you know, that is serious. It means that there is hidden somewhere, like a worm in the fruit, an element of bad will that must be hunted out and destroyed, at any cost, because any weakness on such a point is the source of difficulties that sometimes, later on, become irreparable.

So then the first thing is to be perfectly happy when someone or some circumstance puts you in the conscious presence of a fault in yourself which you did not know. Instead of lamenting, you must rejoice and in this joy must find the strength to get rid of the thing which should not be.

21 March 1958

The Adept

No sorrow exists for one who has completed his journey, who has let fall all cares, who is free in all his parts, who has cast off all bonds.

Those who are heedful strive always and, like swans leaving their lakes, leave one home after another.

Those who amass nothing, who eat moderately, who have perceived the emptiness of all things and who have attained unconditioned liberation, their path is as difficult to trace as that of a bird in the air.

One for whom all desires have passed away and who has perceived the emptiness of all things, who cares little for food, who has attained unconditioned liberation, his path is as difficult to trace as that of a bird in the air.

Even the Gods esteem one whose senses are controlled as horses by the charioteer, one who is purged of all pride and freed from all corruption.

One who fulfils his duty is as immovable as the earth itself. He is as firm as a celestial pillar, pure as an unmuddied lake; and for him the cycle of births is completed.

Calm are the thoughts, the words and the acts of one who has liberated himself by the true knowledge and has achieved a perfect tranquillity.

The greatest among men is he who is not credulous but has the sense of the Uncreated, who has cut all ties, who has destroyed all occasion for rebirth.

Whether village or forest, plain or mountain, wherever the adepts may dwell, that place is always delightful.

Delightful are the forests which are shunned by the multitude. There, the adept, who is free from passion, will find happiness, for he seeks not after pleasure.

There is a very interesting sentence here: "He who is not credulous but has the sense of the Uncreated...."

One who is not credulous — all kinds of things can be understood from this word. The first impression is that it refers to one who does not believe in invisible things without having an experience of them, as distinct from people who follow, for example, a particular religion and have faith in dogmas simply because that is what they have been taught. But he "has the sense of the Uncreated", that is to say, he is in contact with invisible things and knows them as they are, by identity. The Dhammapada has told us, to begin with, that the greatest of men is he who has no faith in what is taught but has a personal experience of things that are not visible, he who is free from all belief and has himself had the experience of invisible things.

Another explanation can also be given: one who is not credulous is he who does not believe in the reality of appearances, in things as we see them, who does not take them for the truth, who knows that these are only misleading appearances and that behind them lies a truth that is to be found and known by personal experience and by identity.

And this makes one reflect on the number of things, the countless number of things that we believe without any personal knowledge, simply because we have been taught that they are like that, or because we are accustomed to think they are like that, or because we are surrounded by people who believe that things are like that. If we look at all the things that we believe and not only believe but assert with an indisputable authority, "This is like this", "That, but of course it is like that", "And

44

this thing, yes, it is so...." In truth, however, we know nothing about it, it is simply because we are in the habit of thinking that they are like that. What are the things that you have experienced personally, with which you have had a direct contact, of which you can at least say with sincerity, "I am convinced that it is like that, because I have experienced it"? Not many.

In reality, if you truly want to have knowledge, you must begin by making a very important study: verify the things that we have been taught, even the most common and the most insignificant. Then you will understand why the text says "the greatest among men", because I do not think that many have made this experiment.

Just to find out the number of things we believe and assert, simply because it is customary to believe and assert them, is indeed a very interesting discovery.

Now go and look into your thought and consciousness for all the things that you assert without proof. You will see!

28 March 1958

The Thousands

Better than a thousand words devoid of meaning is a single meaningful word which can bring tranquillity to one who hears it.

Better than a thousand verses devoid of meaning is a single meaningful verse which can bring tranquillity to one who hears it.

Better than the repetition of a hundred verses devoid of meaning is the repetition of a single verse of the Teaching which can bring tranquillity to one who hears it.

The greatest conqueror is not he who is victorious over thousands of men in battle, but he who is victorious over himself.

The victory that one wins over oneself is of more value than victory over all the peoples.

No god, no Gandharva,[1] nor Mara nor Brahma[2] can change that victory to defeat.

If, month after month, for a hundred years one offers sacrifices by the thousand, and if for a single instant one offers homage to a being full of wisdom, that single homage is worth more than all those countless sacrifices.

If for a hundred years a man tends the flame on Agni's altar, and if, for a single instant, he renders homage to a man who has mastered his nature, this brief homage has more value than all his long devotions.

---

[1] Celestial musician.   [2] The creator of the universe.

Whatever the sacrifices and oblations a man in this world may offer throughout a whole year in order to acquire merit, that is not worth even a quarter of the homage offered to a just man.

For one who is respectful to his elders, four things increase: long life, beauty, happiness and strength.

A single day spent in good conduct and meditation is worth more than a hundred years spent in immorality and dissipation.

A single day of wisdom and meditation is worth more than a hundred years spent in foolishness and dissipation.

A single day of strength and energy is worth more than a hundred years spent in indolence and inertia.

A single day lived in the perception that all things appear and disappear is worth more than a hundred years spent not knowing that they appear and disappear.

A single day spent in contemplation of the path of immortality is worth more than a hundred years lived in ignorance of the path of immortality.

A single day spent in contemplation of the supreme Truth is worth more than a hundred years lived in ignorance of the supreme Truth.

All kinds of different things are gathered here under the same heading. It is an association of words more than an association of ideas. But the central trend is this, that it is preferable to have one moment of sincerity rather than a long life of apparent devotion and that a psychological and spiritual victory over oneself is more important than all external victories.

There is also an interesting reflection, that a victory over oneself is the only victory which is truly safe from the intervention of any god or power of Nature or any instrument of evil. If you have gained self-mastery on one point, that goes beyond the reach of any intervention even from the very highest powers, whether they are gods of the Overmind or any anti-divine powers in the world.

The opening text says that a single word that gives you peace is worth more than thousands of words that have no meaning — this anybody can understand — but it is also said that the word that gives you peace is worth more than thousands of words that can satisfy the mental activity but have no psychological effect on your being.

Indeed, when you have found something which has the power to help you in gaining a victory over your unconsciousness and inertia, you must, till you reach the final result, exhaust all the effects produced by that word or phrase before you look for others.

It is more important to pursue to its end the practice of the effect produced by an idea that one has met somehow, than to try to accumulate in the head a large number of ideas. Ideas may all be very useful in their own time, if they are allowed in at the opportune moment, particularly if you carry to the extreme limit the result of one of those dynamic ideas that are capable of making you win an inner victory. That is to say, one should have for one's chief, if not only aim the practice of what one knows rather than the accumulation in oneself of a knowledge which remains purely theoretical.

So one could sum up: put into practice integrally what you know, only then can you usefully increase your theoretical knowledge.

11 April 1958

Evil

Hasten towards the good, leave behind all evil thoughts, for to do good without enthusiasm is to have a mind which delights in evil.

If one does an evil action, he should not persist in it, he should not delight in it. For full of suffering is the accumulation of evil.

If one does a good action, he should persist in it and take delight in it. Full of happiness is the accumulation of good.

As long as his evil action has not yet ripened, an evil-doer may experience contentment. But when it ripens, the wrong-doer knows unhappiness.

As long as his good action has not yet ripened, one who does good may experience unhappiness. But when it ripens, the good man knows happiness.

Do not treat evil lightly, saying, "That will not touch me." A jar is filled drop by drop; even so the fool fills himself little by little with wickedness.

Do not treat good lightly, saying, "That will not touch me." A jar is filled drop by drop; even so the sage fills himself little by little with goodness.

The merchant who is carrying many precious goods and who has but few companions, avoids dangerous roads; and a man who loves his life is wary of poison. Even so should one act regarding evil.

A hand that has no wound can carry poison with impunity; act likewise, for evil cannot touch the righteous man.

If you offend one who is pure, innocent and defenceless, the insult will fall back on you, as if you threw dust against the wind.

Some are reborn here on earth, evil-doers go to the worlds of Niraya,[1] the just go to the heavenly worlds, but those who have freed themselves from all desire attain Nirvana.

Neither in the skies, nor in the depths of the ocean, nor in the rocky caves, nowhere upon earth does there exist a place where a man can find refuge from his evil actions.

Neither in the skies, nor in the depths of the ocean, nor in the rocky caves, nowhere upon earth does there exist a place where a man can hide from death.

People have the habit of dealing lightly with thoughts that come. And the atmosphere is full of thoughts of all kinds which do not in fact belong to anybody in particular, which move perpetually from one person to another, very freely, much too freely, because there are very few people who can keep their thoughts under control.

When you take up the Buddhist discipline to learn how to control your thoughts, you make very interesting discoveries. You try to observe your thoughts. Instead of letting them pass freely, sometimes even letting them enter your head and establish themselves in a quite inopportune way, you look at them, observe them and you realise with stupefaction that in the space of

---

[1] Hell; the state of suffering.

a few seconds there passes through the head a series of absolutely improbable thoughts that are altogether harmful.

You believe you are so good, so kind, so well disposed and always full of good feelings. You wish no harm to anybody, you wish only good — all that you tell yourself complacently. But if you look at yourself sincerely as you are thinking, you notice that you have in your head a collection of thoughts which are sometimes frightful and of which you were not at all aware.

For example, your reactions when something has not pleased you: how eager you are to send your friends, relatives, acquaintances, everyone, to the devil! How you wish them all kinds of unpleasant things, without even being aware of it! And how you say, "Ah, that will teach him to be like that!" And when you criticise, you say, "He must be made aware of his faults." And when someone has not acted according to your ideas, you say, "He will be punished for it!" and so on.

You do not know it because you do not look at yourself in the act of thinking. Sometimes you know it, when it becomes a little too strong. But when the thing simply passes through, you hardly notice it — it comes, it enters, it leaves. Then you find out that if you truly want to be pure and wholly on the side of the Truth, then that requires a vigilance, a sincerity, a self-observation, a self-control which are not common. You begin to realise that it is difficult to be truly sincere.

You flatter yourself that you have nothing but good feelings and good intentions and that whatever you do, you do for the sake of what is good — yes, so long as you are conscious and have control, but the moment you are not very attentive, all kinds of things happen within you of which you are not at all conscious and which are not very pretty.

If you want to clean your house thoroughly, you must be vigilant for a long time, for a very long time and especially not believe that you have reached the goal, like that, at one stroke, because one day you happened to decide that you would be on the right side. That is of course a very essential and important point, but it must be followed by a good many other days when you have to keep a strict guard on yourself so as not to belie your resolution.

4 April 1958

Punishment

All tremble when faced with punishment; all fear death. Seeing others as ourselves, do not strike, do not cause another to strike.

All tremble when faced with punishment; life is dear to all. Seeing others as ourselves, do not strike, do not cause another to strike.

Whosoever hurts creatures eager for happiness for the sake of his own happiness, nevertheless will not obtain it after his death.

Whosoever does not hurt creatures eager for happiness for the sake of his own happiness, will obtain it after death.

Never speak harsh words to anyone, for they will be returned to you. Angry words cause suffering and one who utters them will bear them in return.

If you remain as silent as a broken gong, you have already entered Nirvana, for violence no longer abides in you.

As the cowherd, with his stick, drives the herd to pasture, so old age and death drive the life out of all living beings.

The fool does evil without knowing it; he is consumed and tormented by his actions as by a fire.

One who does harm to one who does none, one who offends one who offends not, will soon suffer one of the ten states that follow:

He will endure intense pain, he will suffer disastrous losses and terrible injury, serious illness, madness.

Or he will come in conflict with authority, he will be the object of gross calumny, he will lose his near ones or his possessions.

Or else fire will destroy his dwelling-place; and at the time of the dissolution of his body he will be reborn in Hell.

Neither going naked or with matted hair, nor remaining dirty, nor fasting, nor sleeping on the bare ground, nor smearing the body with ashes, nor the practice of ascetic postures, can purify the mortal who has not cast away all doubt.

However richly he is dressed, if a man cultivates tranquillity of mind, if he is calm, resigned, master of himself, pure, if he does no harm to any creature, he is a Brahmin, he is an ascetic, he is a Bhikkhu.

Is there in this world a man beyond reproach that merits no blame, as a thoroughbred needs no blow from the whip?

Like a spirited horse, be quick and eager for the goal. By trust, virtue, energy, meditation, the quest for truth, perfection of knowledge and conduct, by faith destroy in you all suffering.

Those who build waterways lead the water where they want; those who make arrows straighten them; carpenters shape their wood; the sage controls himself.

One has the impression that these things were written for rather primitive people. The series of calamities that will befall you if you do harm is quite amusing.

It would seem — provided of course that this is an exact record of the words that the Buddha spoke — that he must have changed the terms of his talks according to his audience and if he had to do with rustic people without education, he would speak a very material language with very practical and concrete comparisons so that they might understand him. There is a considerable difference of level in these verses. Some have become very famous, as, for example, the last verse here, where it is said that the artisan shapes his material to achieve what he has to do, and this striking conclusion: the sage controls himself.

Truly one has the impression that human mentality has progressed since that age. Thought has become more complex, psychology more profound, to the extent that these arguments appear almost puerile. But when we mean to practise them, then we realise that we have remained almost on the same level, and that if thought has progressed, practice, far from being better, seems to have become worse. And here there is a childlike simplicity, something rather healthy, an absence of perversion that unfortunately the human race no longer possesses.

There was a moral healthiness in those days which has now completely disappeared. These arguments make you smile, but the practice of what is taught here is much more difficult now than it was at that time. A kind of hypocrisy, pretension, underhand duplicity seems to have taken possession of the human mind and especially its way of being, and men have learnt to deceive themselves in a most pernicious way.

In those times, one could say, "Don't do harm, you will be punished"; hearts were simple and the mind as well, and one said, "Yes, it is better not to do harm, because I will be punished." But now, with an ironical smile, you say, "Oh! I shall surely find a way to avoid punishment."

Mental capacity seems to have grown, mental power seems to have developed, men seem to be much more capable of playing with ideas, of having mental command over all principles, but at the same time they have lost the simple and healthy candour of people who lived closer to Nature and knew less how to play with ideas. Thus humanity as a whole seems to have reached a very dangerous turning-point. Those who are trying to find a solution to the general corruption preach a return to the simplicity of yore, but of course that is quite impossible: you cannot go back.

We must go farther on, we must advance, climb greater heights and go beyond the arid search for pleasure and personal welfare, not through fear of punishment, even punishment after death, but through the development of a new sense of beauty, a thirst for truth and light, through understanding that it is only by widening yourself, illumining yourself, setting yourself ablaze with the ardour for progress, that you can find both integral peace and enduring happiness.

One must rise up and widen — rise up... and widen.

18 April 1958

Old Age

Why this joy, this gladness, when the world is forever burning? O you who are enveloped in shadows, why do you not seek the light?

See then this poor decorated form, this mass of corruptible elements, of infirmities and vain desires in which nothing is lasting or stable.

This fragile body is but a nest of misery, of decrepitude and corruption; for life ends in death.

What pleasure is there in contemplating these white bones strewn like gourds in autumn?

In this fortress made of bone and covered with flesh and blood, only pride and jealousy, dissolution and death are established.

Even the gorgeous chariots of kings are worn out in the end. It is the same with this body which at last is worn out with age; but the true Law is never worn out and so one sage can pass it on to another.

The ignorant man grows older like a bullock; his weight increases but not his intelligence.

Many times have I passed in vain through the cycle of births in search of the builder of this house. And how painful is this cycle of births!

At last, I have found you, builder; never again shall you build this house that is my body. All the beams are shattered and the ridge of the roof has crumbled.

My liberated mind has attained the extinction of all desires.

Those who have not lived a life of self-control and who, in their youth, have not known how to gather the true riches, perish like aged herons beside a lake with no fish.

Those who have not lived a life of self-control and who, in their youth, have not known how to gather the true riches are like shattered bows; they grieve for their lost strength.

There is one thing certain which is not clearly stated here, but which is at least as important as all the rest. It is this, that there is an old age much more dangerous and much more real than the amassing of years: the incapacity to grow and progress.

As soon as you stop advancing, as soon as you stop progressing, as soon as you cease to better yourself, cease to gain and grow, cease to transform yourself, you truly become old, that is to say, you go downhill towards disintegration.

There are young people who are old and there are old people who are young. If you carry in you this flame for progress and transformation, if you are ready to leave everything behind so that you may advance with an alert step, if you are always open to a new progress, a new improvement, a new transformation, then you are eternally young. But if you sit back satisfied with what has been accomplished, if you have the feeling that you have reached your goal and you have nothing left to do but enjoy the fruit of your efforts, then already more than half your body is in the tomb: it is decrepitude and the true death.

Everything that has been done is always nothing compared with what remains to be done.

Do not look behind. Look ahead, always ahead and go forward always.

25 April 1958

58

The Ego

If a man holds himself dear, let him guard himself closely. The sage should watch through one of the three vigils of his existence (youth, maturity, or old age).

One should begin by establishing oneself in the right path; then, one will be able to advise others. Thus the sage is above all reproach.

If one puts into practice what he teaches to others, being master of himself, he can very well guide others; for in truth it is difficult to master oneself.

In truth, one is one's own master, for what other master can there be? By mastering oneself, one acquires a mastery which is difficult to achieve.

The evil done by himself, originated by himself, emanating from him, crushes the fool as the diamond crushes a hard gem.

Just as the creeper clings to the Sal tree, even so one entrapped by his own evil actions does to himself the harm his enemy would wish him.

It is so easy to do oneself wrong and harm, but how difficult it is to do what is good and profitable!

The fool who, because of his wrong views, rejects the teachings of the adepts, the Noble Ones and the Just, brings about his own destruction, as the fruit of the bamboo kills the plant.

Doing evil, one harms oneself; avoiding evil, one purifies oneself; purity and impurity depend on ourselves; no one can purify another.

No man should neglect his supreme Good to follow another, however great. Knowing clearly what is his best line of conduct, he should not swerve from it.

The question here seems to be more about egoism than ego.

Egoism is a relatively easy thing to correct, because everyone knows what it is. It is easy to discover, easy to correct, if one truly wants to do it and is bent on it.

But the ego is much more difficult to seize, because, in fact, to realise what the ego is one must already be out of it, otherwise one cannot find it out. You are wholly moulded from it, from head to foot, from the outermost to the innermost, from the physical to the spiritual, you are steeped in ego. It is mixed with everything and you are not aware of what it is. You must have already conquered it, come out of it, freed yourself from it, at least partially, at least in some little corner of your being somewhere, in order to realise what the ego is.

The ego is what helps us to individualise ourselves and what prevents us from becoming divine. It is like that. Put that together and you will find the ego. Without the ego, as the world is organised, there would be no individual, and with the ego the world cannot become divine.

It would be logical to conclude, "Well, let us first of all become conscious individuals and then we shall send away the ego and become divine." Only, when we have become conscious individuals, we have grown so accustomed to living with our ego that we are no longer able to discern it and much labour is needed to become aware of its presence.

On the other hand, everyone knows what egoism is. When you want to pull everything towards you and other people do not interest you, that is called egoism; when you put yourself at the centre of the universe and all things exist only in relation to you, that is egoism. But it is very obvious, one must be blind not to see that one is egoistic. Everybody is a little egoistic, more or less, and at least a certain proportion of egoism is normally acceptable; but even in ordinary life, when one is a little too egoistic, well, one receives knocks on the nose, because, since everyone is egoistic, no one much likes egoism in others.

It is taken for granted, it is part of public morality. Yes, one must be a little bit egoistic, not too much, so it is not conspicuous! On the other hand, nobody speaks of the ego, because nobody knows it. It is such an intimate companion that one does not even recognise its existence; and yet so long as it is there one will never have the divine consciousness.

The ego is what makes one conscious of being separate from others. If there were no ego, you would not perceive that you are a person separate from others. You would have the impression that you are a small part of a whole, a very small part of a very great whole. On the other hand, every one of you is most certainly quite conscious of being a separate person. Well, it is the ego that gives you this impression. As long as you are conscious in this way, it means that you have an ego.

When you begin to be aware that everything is yourself, and that this is only a very small point in the midst of thousands and thousands of other points of the same person that you are everywhere, when you feel that you are yourself in everything and that there is no separation, then you know that you are on the way towards having no more ego.

There even comes a time when it is impossible to conceive oneself and say, "It is not I", for even to express it in this way, to say that the All is you, that you are the All or that you are the Divine or that the Divine is you, proves that something still remains.

There is a moment — this happens in a flash and can hardly stay — when it is the All that thinks, it is the All that knows, it is the All that feels, it is the All that lives. There is not even... not even the impression that... you have reached that point.

Then it is all right. But until then, there is still a little remnant of ego somewhere; usually it is the part which looks on, the witness that looks on.

So do not assert that you have no more ego. It is not accurate. Say you are on the way towards having no more ego, that is the only correct thing to say.

I do not believe that it has happened to you, has it? — not yet! And yet it is indispensable, if you truly intend to know what the supramental is. If you are a candidate for supermanhood, you must resolve to dispense with your ego, to go beyond it, for as long as you keep it with you, the supermind will be for you something unknown and inaccessible.

But if through effort, through discipline, through progressive mastery, you surmount your ego and go beyond it, even if only in the tiniest part of your being, this acts like the opening of a small window somewhere, and by looking carefully through the window, you will be able to glimpse the supermind. And that is a promise. When you glimpse it, you find it so beautiful that you immediately want to get rid of all the rest... of the ego!

Please note that I am not saying that you must be totally free from all ego in order to have a glimpse of the supramental; for then that would be something almost impossible. No, to be free from ego, just a little bit somewhere, in some corner of your being, even only a little corner of the mind; if it is the mind and the vital, it is well and good, but if by chance — oh! not by chance — if by repeated efforts you have entered into contact with your psychic being, then the door is wide open. Through the psychic you can suddenly have a very clear and beautiful vision of what the supermind is, only a vision, not a realisation. That is the great way out. But even without going so far as this beautiful realisation, the psychic realisation, if you succeed in liberating some part of your mind or your vital, that makes a kind of hole in the door, a keyhole; through this keyhole you have a glimpse, just a little glimpse. And that is already very attractive, very interesting.

2 May 1958

The World

Do not follow the way of evil. Do not cultivate indolence of mind. Do not choose wrong views. Do not be of those who linger in the world.

Arise. Cast off negligence. Follow the teaching of wisdom. The sage knows happiness in this world and the other.

Follow the teaching of wisdom and not that of evil. The sage knows happiness in this world and the other.

One who looks upon the world as a bubble or a mirage, Yama the King of Death cannot find him.

Come, look upon the world as the brightly-coloured chariot of a Raja, which attracts the foolish, but where, in truth, there is nothing attractive.

One who, having been negligent, becomes vigilant, illumines the earth like the moon coming forth from behind the clouds.

One whose good actions efface the evil he has done, illumines the earth like the moon coming forth from behind the clouds.

The world is wrapped in darkness and few are those who find their way, who, like a bird escaping from a net, soar up towards heaven.

The swans take the path of the sun. Those who possess occult powers fly through the air. The sages leave this world after defeating Mara and his army of evil.

No evil is impossible to him who transgresses one law of the Doctrine, who utters falsehood and who disdains the higher world.

In truth, misers do not attain to the world of the gods and fools do not know the happiness of giving. But the sage delights in giving and thus knows happiness in the other world.

Rather than ruling the earth, rather than reaching heaven, rather than reigning over the worlds, it is better to enter the upward current.

There are four pieces of advice here which I would like to retain for our meditation. "Do not cultivate indolence of mind." "Do not choose wrong views" — unfortunately this is something one does all the time. And, "Arise. Cast off negligence."

The world has been so made — at least up to now, let us hope that it will not be so for much longer — that, spontaneously, a man who is not cultured, when he is brought into contact with ideas, always chooses wrong ideas.

And a child who is not educated always chooses bad company. It is a thing I experience constantly and concretely. If you keep a child in a special atmosphere and if, from a very early age, you instill in him a special atmosphere, a special purity, he has a chance of not making a wrong choice. But a child who is taken from the world as it is and is placed in a society where there are good and bad elements will go straight to those who can spoil him, teach him wrong things, that is to say, towards the worst company.

A man who has no intellectual culture, if you give him some mixed ideas, just at random, to choose from, he will always choose the stupid ones; because, as Sri Aurobindo has told us, this is a world of falsehood, of ignorance and an effort is needed, an aspiration; one must come in contact with one's inmost being — a conscious and luminous contact — if one is to distinguish the true from the false, the good influence from the bad. If you let yourself go, you sink into a hole.

Things are like that because what rules the world — oh! let us put it in the past tense, so that it becomes true — what ruled the world was falsehood and ignorance.

In fact, for the moment, it is still like that; one should have no illusions about it. But perhaps with a great effort and great vigilance we shall be able to make it otherwise... soon — the "perhaps" is for "soon".

Surely it will come one day, but we want it soon, and that is why the last two recommendations please me: "Arise. Cast off negligence."

9 May 1958

The Awakened One (The Buddha)

He whose victory has never been surpassed nor even equalled — which path can lead to Him, the Pathless, the Awakened One who dwells within the Infinite?

One in whom there is neither greed nor desire, how can he be led astray? Which path can lead to Him, the Pathless, the Awakened One who dwells within the Infinite?

Even the gods envy the sages given to meditation, the Awakened Ones, the Vigilant who live with delight in renunciation and solitude.

It is difficult to attain to human birth. It is difficult to live this mortal life. It is difficult to obtain the good fortune of hearing the True Doctrine. And difficult indeed is the advent of the Awakened Ones.

Abstain from evil; cultivate good and purify your mind. This is the teaching of the Awakened Ones.

Of all ascetic practices patience is the best; of all states the most perfect is Nirvana, say the Awakened Ones. He who harms others is not a monk. He who oppresses others is not a true ascetic.

Neither to offend, nor to do wrong to anyone, to practise discipline according to the Law, to be moderate in eating, to live in seclusion, and to merge oneself in the higher consciousness, this is the teaching of the Awakened Ones.

Even a rain of gold would not be able to quench the thirst of desire, for it is insatiable and the origin of sorrows. This the sage knows.

Even the pleasures of heaven are without savour for the sage. The disciple of the Buddha, of the Perfectly Awakened One, rejoices only in the extinction of all desire.

Impelled by fear, men seek refuge in many places, in the mountains, in the forests, in the groves, in sanctuaries.

But this is not a safe refuge; this is not the supreme refuge. Coming to this refuge does not save a man from all sufferings.

One who takes refuge in the Buddha, in the Dhamma[1] and the Sangha,[2] with perfect knowledge, perceives the Four Noble Truths:

Suffering, the origin of suffering, the cessation of suffering and the Noble Eightfold Path which leads to cessation of suffering.

In truth, this is the sure refuge, this is the sovereign refuge. To choose this refuge is to be liberated from all suffering.

It is difficult to meet the Perfectly Noble One. Such a being is not born everywhere. And where such a sage is born, those around him live in happiness.

Happy is the birth of the Buddhas, happy the teaching of the true Law. Happy is the harmony of the Sangha, happy the discipline of the United.

---

[1] The True Doctrine.
[2] The community; the order of the Great Ones and the order of the monks.

> *One cannot measure the merit of the man who reveres*
> *those who are worthy of reverence, whether the Buddha*
> *or his disciples, those who are free from all desire and all*
> *error, those who have overcome all obstacles and who*
> *have crossed beyond suffering and grief.*

This concerns the Four Truths and the Eightfold Path that lead to the annihilation of suffering. Here are the details given in the text:

The Four Noble Truths are:

(1) Life — taken in the sense of ordinary life, the life of ignorance and falsehood — is indissolubly linked with suffering: suffering of the body and suffering of the mind.

(2) The cause of suffering is desire, which is caused by ignorance of the nature of separative life.

(3) There is a way to escape from suffering, to put an end to pain.

(4) This liberation is obtained by following the discipline of the Eightfold Path which gradually purifies the mind from the Ignorance. The fourth Truth is called the method of the Eightfold Path.

The Noble Path consists in a training in the following eight stages:

(1) *Correct seeing.* To see things as they are, that is to say, a pure, accurate vision, the best vision.

Three conditions characterise existence: pain, impermanence, the absence of a fixed ego. So the Dhammapada says. But it is not quite that, it is rather the absence of a fixed, durable and separate personality in the psychological aggregate, the lack of a true continuity in the personal consciousness. It is for this reason that, for example, in the ordinary state one cannot remember one's past lives nor have the sense of a conscious continuity through all one's lives.

The first point then is to see correctly, and to see correctly is to see that pain is associated with ordinary life, that all things are impermanent and that there is no continuity in the personal consciousness.

(2) *Correct intention or desire.* But the same word "desire" should not have been used, because we have just been told that we should not have desire. It is rather "correct aspiration". The word "desire" should be replaced by "aspiration".

"To be freed from attachments and to have kind thoughts for everything that exists." To be constantly in a state of kindness. To wish the best for all, always.

(3) *Correct speech that hurts none.* Never speak uselessly and scrupulously avoid all malevolent speech.

(4) *Correct behaviour — peaceful, honest.* From all points of view, not only materially, but morally, mentally. Mental honesty is one of the most difficult things to achieve.

(5) *Correct way of living. Not to cause harm or danger to any creature.* This is relatively easy to understand. There are people who carry this principle to the extreme, against all common sense. Those who put a handkerchief to their mouths, for example, so as not to swallow germs, who have the path in front of them swept so as not to step on an insect. This seems to me a little excessive, because the whole of life as it is at present is made up of destruction. But if you understand the text correctly, it means that one must avoid all possibility of doing harm, one must not deliberately endanger any creature. You can include here all living creatures and if you extend this care and this kindness to everything that lives in the universe, it will be very favourable to your inner growth.

(6) *Correct effort.* Do not make useless efforts for useless things, rather keep all the energy of your effort to conquer ignorance and free yourself from falsehood. That you can never do too much.

(7) The seventh principle comes to confirm the sixth: *correct vigilance.* You must have an active and vigilant mind. Do not live in a half-somnolence, half-unconsciousness — usually in life you let yourself go, come what may! This is what everyone does. Now and then you wake up and you realise that you have wasted your

69

time; then you make a big effort only to fall back again, a minute later, into indolence. It would be better to have something less vehement but more constant.

(8) And finally, *correct contemplation*. Egoless thought concentrated on the essence of things, on the inmost truth and on the goal to be attained.

How often there is a kind of emptiness in the course of life, an unoccupied moment, a few minutes, sometimes more. And what do you do? Immediately you try to distract yourself, and you invent some foolishness or other to pass your time. That is a common fact. All men, from the youngest to the oldest, spend most of their time in trying not to be bored. Their pet aversion is boredom and the way to escape from boredom is to act foolishly.

Well, there is a better way than that — to remember.

When you have a little time, whether it is one hour or a few minutes, tell yourself, "At last, I have some time to concentrate, to collect myself, to relive the purpose of my life, to offer myself to the True and the Eternal." If you took care to do this each time you are not harassed by outer circumstances, you would find out that you were advancing very quickly on the path. Instead of wasting your time in chattering, in doing useless things, reading things that lower the consciousness — to choose only the best cases, I am not speaking of other imbecilities which are much more serious — instead of trying to make yourself giddy, to make time, that is already so short, still shorter only to realise at the end of your life that you have lost three-quarters of your chance — then you want to put in double time, but that does not work — it is better to be moderate, balanced, patient, quiet, but never to lose an opportunity that is given to you, that is to say, to utilise for the true purpose the unoccupied moment before you.

When you have nothing to do, you become restless, you run about, you meet friends, you take a walk, to speak only of the best; I am not referring to things that are obviously not to be done. Instead of that, sit down quietly before the sky, before the sea or under trees, whatever is possible (here you have all of them) and try to realise one of these things — to understand why you live, to learn how you must live, to ponder over what you want to do and what should be done, what is the best way of escaping from the ignorance and falsehood and pain in which you live.

16 May 1958

Happiness

Among those who hate, happy are we to live without hatred. Among men who hate, let us live free from hatred.

Among those who suffer, happy are we to live without suffering. Among men who suffer, let us live free from suffering.

Among those who are full of greed, happy are we to live without greed. Among the greedy, let us live free from greed.

Happy indeed are we who own nothing. We shall feed upon delight like the radiant gods.

Victory engenders enmity, and one who is vanquished lives in distress. The man of peace lives in gladness, disdaining both victory and defeat.

There is no greater fire than lust, no greater misfortune than hatred. There is no greater misery than existence, no bliss greater than the Supreme Peace.

Hunger is the worst malady; existence is the worst calamity. One who has understood this realises that Nirvana is the Supreme Happiness.

Health is the greatest acquisition, contentment the greatest treasure. A faithful friend is the best companion and Nirvana the Supreme Happiness.

Having tasted the sweetness of solitude and the Supreme Peace, a man is liberated from suffering and evil, for he partakes of the sweetness of devotion to the Truth.

It is good to contemplate the Noble Ones; to live near them is an endless happiness. One could be always happy by avoiding the sight of fools.

One who frequents fools is bound to suffer long; the company of fools is as painful as that of enemies. To live in the company of the sages is to share the happiness of one who lives among his kinsmen.

Seek therefore the company of the sage who is steadfast, learned, wise, devoted and noble. Follow the example of such a good and wise being, as the moon follows the path of the stars.

One of these verses is very beautiful. We could translate it like this: "Happy is he who possesses nothing, he will partake of the delight of the radiant gods." To possess nothing does not at all mean not to make use of anything, not to have anything at one's disposal. "Happy is he who possesses nothing": he is someone who has no sense of possession, who can make use of things when they come to him, knowing that they are not his, that they belong to the Supreme, and who, for the same reason, does not regret it when things leave him; he finds it quite natural that the Lord who gave him these things should take them away from him for others to enjoy. Such a man finds equal joy in the use of things as in the absence of things. When you have them at your disposal, you receive them as a gift of Grace and when they leave you, when they have been taken away from you, you live in the joy of destitution. For it is the sense of ownership that makes you cling to things, makes you their slave, otherwise one could live in constant joy and in the ceaseless movement of things that come and go and pass, that bring with them both the sense of fullness when they are there and, when they go, the delight of detachment.

Delight! Delight means to live in the Truth, to live in communion with Eternity, with the true Life, the Light that never fails.

Delight means to be free, free with the true Freedom, the Freedom of the constant, invariable union with the Divine Will.

Gods are those that are immortal, who are not bound to the vicissitudes of material life in all its narrowness, pettiness, unreality and falsehood.

Gods are those who are turned to the Light, who live in the Power and the Knowledge; that is what the Buddha means, he does not mean the gods of religion. They are beings who have the divine nature, who may live in human bodies, but free from ignorance and falsehood.

When you no longer possess anything, you can become as vast as the universe.

23 May 1958

Pleasure

One who gives himself entirely to what is unprofitable, who does not give himself to what is profitable, who sacrifices true knowledge for the sake of pleasure, will envy those who have chosen the path of self-knowledge.

Therefore do not seek after pleasure, much less what is unpleasant, for it is painful to be deprived of what is pleasing and equally painful to see what is unpleasant.

Therefore one should hold nothing dear, for the loss of what one loves is painful. No bondage exists for those who have neither love nor hatred.

What is pleasing gives rise to grief; what is pleasing gives rise to fear. One who is freed from what is pleasing, who feels no grief, what has he to fear?

Affection gives rise to grief; affection gives rise to fear. One who is freed from affection, who feels no grief, what has he to fear?

Attachment gives rise to grief; attachment gives rise to fear. One who is freed from attachment, who feels no grief, what has he to fear?

Desire gives rise to grief; desire gives rise to fear. One who is freed from desire, who feels no grief, what has he to fear?

Craving gives rise to grief; craving gives rise to fear. One who is freed from craving, who feels no grief, what has he to fear?

One holds dear a man who acts rightly, possesses intuition, who is righteous and knows the Truth, who fulfils his duty.

One who aspires to the ineffable Peace, one whose mind is awakened, whose thoughts are not entangled in the net of desire, that one is said to be "bound upstream" (towards perfection).

Just as, after a long absence, a man returning safely home is received by his kinsmen and friends who welcome him, even so it is with one who acts rightly; when he passes from this world to the other, his own good actions welcome him like a kinsman.

It always seems to me that the reasons usually given for becoming wise are poor reasons: "Don't do this, it will bring you suffering; don't do that, it will give birth to fear in you"... and the consciousness dries up more and more, it hardens, because it is afraid of grief, afraid of pain.

I think it would be better to say that there is a certain state of consciousness — which one can acquire by aspiration and a persistent inner effort — in which joy is unmixed and light shadowless, where all possibility of fear disappears. It is the state in which one does not live for oneself but where whatever one does, whatever one feels, all movements are an offering made to the Supreme, in an absolute trust, freeing oneself of all responsibility for oneself, handing over to Him all this burden which is no longer a burden.

It is an inexpressible joy not to have any responsibility for oneself, no longer to think of oneself. It is so dull and monotonous and insipid to be thinking of oneself, to be worrying about what to do and what not to do, what will be good for you and what will be bad for you, what to shun and what to pursue — oh, how wearisome it is! But when one lives like this, quite open, like a flower blossoming in the sun before the Supreme Consciousness, the Supreme Wisdom, the Supreme Light, the Supreme Love, which knows all, which can do all, which takes charge of you and you have no more worries — that is the ideal condition.

And why is it not done?

One does not think of it, one forgets to do it, the old habits come back. And above all, behind, hidden somewhere in the inconscient or even in the subconscient, there is this insidious doubt that whispers in your ear: "Oh! if you are not careful, some misfortune will happen to you. If you forget to watch over yourself, you do not know what may happen" — and you are so silly, so silly, so obscure, so stupid that you listen and you begin to pay attention to yourself and everything is ruined.

You have to begin all over again to infuse into your cells a little wisdom, a little common sense and learn once more not to worry.

30 May 1958

Anger

One should cast away anger, one should reject pride, one should break all bonds. One who is not attached to name or form, who possesses nothing, is delivered from suffering.

Whosoever masters rising anger, as one who controls a moving chariot, that one indeed is worthy of being called a good charioteer. Others merely hold the reins.

Oppose anger with serenity, evil with good; conquer a miser by generosity and a liar by the truth.

Speak the truth; do not give way to anger; give the little you possess to one who asks of you; by these three attributes, men can approach the gods.

The sages who are void of violence, who are always in control of their senses, attain that imperishable state where pain is no more.

Those who are always vigilant and who discipline themselves day and night, whose minds are always turned towards Nirvana, will see their impurities disappear for ever.

Not only today but since ancient times, they have always been criticised, those who remain silent, those who speak much and those who speak little. None here below escapes criticism.

There has never been and never will be, nor is there now, one who receives only blame or only praise.

78

If a man is praised by the sages, who have observed him day after day, for being intelligent, without reproach, endowed with knowledge and virtue, who then would dare to blame him who is as pure as gold? Even the gods and Brahma praise him.

Be on your guard against the wrath of the body. Control your actions, and leaving behind wrong ways of acting, practise perfect conduct in action.

Be on your guard against wrath in speech. Control your words, and leaving behind wrong ways of speaking, practise good conduct in speech.

Be on your guard against wrath of mind. Control your thoughts, and leaving behind wrong ways of thinking, practise good conduct in thought.

The sages whose actions are controlled, whose words are controlled and whose thoughts are controlled, they in truth are perfectly controlled.

I suggest that every one of you should try — oh! not for long, just for one hour a day — to say nothing but the absolutely indispensable words. Not one more, not one less.

Take one hour of your life, the one which is most convenient for you, and during that time observe yourself closely and say only the absolutely indispensable words.

At the outset, the first difficulty will be to know what is absolutely indispensable and what is not. It is already a study in itself and every day you will do better.

Next, you will see that so long as one says nothing, it is not difficult to remain absolutely silent, but as soon as you begin to speak, always or almost always you say two or three or ten or twenty useless words which it was not at all necessary to say.

I give you this as an exercise till next Friday. We shall see how you succeed. You may, at the end of the week, on Friday, give me a brief note telling me how far you have succeeded — those who have tried. That's all.

6 June 1958

Impurity

Now you are like a withered leaf; the messengers of Yama await you. It is the eve of your departure, and you have made no provision for your journey!

Quickly make for yourself an island of refuge, strive hard and become wise. When you are cleansed and purified of all impurity, you will enter the heavenly home of the Noble Ones.

Now your days are numbered, you are in the presence of the God of death. You have no resting-place on the road, no provision for the journey.

Quickly make for yourself an island of refuge, strive hard and become wise. When you are cleansed and purified of all impurity, you will be reborn no more, you will no more be subject to decay.

Just as the smith refines the silver, so also, little by little from moment to moment, the wise man purifies himself of his impurities.

When rust appears on iron, the iron itself is corrupted by it. So also, a man's evil actions corrupt him and lead him to his doom.

Lack of repetition impairs the effect of mantras.[1] Neglect impairs the solidity of houses. Indolence impairs the beauty of the body. Lack of attention is the downfall of one who watches.

[1] Words charged with spiritual power.

Misconduct is the taint of a woman. Meanness is the taint of one who gives. Wrong-doing is a taint in this world and the other.

The greatest of all taints is ignorance. Cleanse yourselves of that taint alone and you will be free of all taints, O Bhikkhus.

Life is easy for one who is impudent as a crow, malicious, boastful, presumptuous and corrupt.

Life is hard for the modest one who seeks purity, who is detached, unassuming and whose judgment is correct.

Already in this world he is uprooted, the one who destroys life, who lies, who takes what he has not been given, who covets the wife of another and who is addicted to drink.

Know that evil things are difficult to master. Let not cravings and wickedness subject you to endless suffering.

Each one gives according to his faith or his liking; if you are discontented with the food and drink offered by another, you will not achieve concentration by night or by day.

But the one who uproots and destroys in himself the very root of such a feeling of resentment, achieves concentration by night and by day.

There is no fire like the fire of craving, no grip like that of hatred. There is no snare like that of delusion, no torrent like desire.

It is easy to see the faults of others, but difficult to perceive our own shortcomings. We winnow the faults of

82

*others like chaff, but we hide our own like the wily
gambler concealing his foul throw.*

*One who always criticises the faults of others and is irri-
tated by them, far from becoming free of faults, increases
his own vices.*

*There is no track in the sky, no Samana[2] outside the
true path. Man delights in vanity. The Tathagatas[3] have
overcome these obstacles.*

*There is no track in the sky, no Samana outside the true
path. No conditioned thing can last, but the Buddhas
remain for ever immutable.*

I have read your notes on the control of speech. Some have tried
very seriously. I am happy with the result. I believe it will be good
for everyone if you continue.

Someone has written me something which is very true: that
when one begins, one has no reason to stop, one begins with one
hour a day, but this becomes a kind of necessity, a habit and one
continues quite naturally.

If your exercise truly has this result, then it will be an excellent
thing.

We can select three things from what I have read this evening.
The first is that you must persist in what you do if you want to
get a result. The Dhammapada tells us, for example, that if you
have a mantra and do not repeat it sufficiently, there is no use in
having it and that if you are inattentive, you lose the benefit of
vigilance, and that if you do not continue in the good habits that
you acquire, they are useless — that is to say, you must persevere.
As for example, with the exercise which I asked you to do last

---

[2] Ascetic.
[3] The Buddhas who, according to tradition, came on earth to reveal the eternal Truth.

time; I asked you to do it with the idea that if you form the habit of doing it, that will help you much in overcoming your difficulties.

Already someone has told me, quite rightly, that while practising this half-silence, or at any rate this continence of speech, one achieves quite naturally the mastery of numerous difficulties in one's character and also one avoids a great many frictions and misunderstandings. This is true.

Another point to remember from our reading concerns impurity and the Dhammapada gives the example of bad will and wrong action. Wrong action, says our text, is a taint in this world as well as in others. In the next verse it is said that there is no greater impurity than ignorance, that is to say, ignorance is considered as the essential, the central fault, which urgently needs to be corrected, and what is called ignorance is not simply not knowing things, not having the superficial knowledge of things, it means forgetting the very reason of our existence, the truth that has to be discovered.

There was a third thing?... Yes, you must not cherish the illusion that if you want to follow the straight path, if you are modest, if you seek purity, if you are disinterested, if you want to lead a solitary existence and have a clear judgment, things will become easy.... It is quite the contrary! When you begin to advance towards inner and outer perfection, the difficulties start at the same time.

I have very often heard people saying, "Oh! now that I am trying to be good, everybody seems to be bad to me!" But this is precisely to teach you that one should not be good with an interested motive, one should not be good so that others will be good to you — one must be good for the sake of being good.

It is always the same lesson: one must do as well as one can, the best one can, but without expecting a result, without doing it with a view to the result. Just this attitude, to expect a reward for a good action — to become good because one thinks that this will make life easier — takes away all value from the good action.

You must be good for the love of goodness, you must be just

84

for the love of justice, you must be pure for the love of purity and you must be disinterested for the love of disinterestedness; then you are sure to advance on the way.

13 June 1958

The Just Man

A man is not just if he judges arbitrarily. The wise man is one who distinguishes the just from the unjust, who judges others in full knowledge according to law and equity; this guardian of the Law is called a just man.

The sage is not the man who speaks most. The man who is compassionate, friendly, fearless, is called a sage.

It is not by much speaking that the Doctrine is upheld; but he who has studied the Doctrine, even a little, and mentally realised it, he alone upholds it. He does not neglect it.

A man is not a Thera[1] because his hair is grey. He is ripe in years but he has aged fruitlessly.

But one who possesses the truth, virtue, non-violence and self-mastery, who is free from all impurity, who is wise, is indeed a Thera.

Neither eloquence nor a beautiful appearance grace a man who is jealous, selfish, deceitful. But one in whom such faults are completely uprooted and destroyed, that wise man is fully graced by them.

As for the man who is undisciplined and untruthful, his shaven head does not make him an ascetic. Full of desire and greed, how can he be a Samana?

He who is purged of all evil, both great and small, can be called a Samana, for he is purified of all evil.

[1] A senior monk.

A man is not a Bhikkhu simply because he takes alms for his food. The observance of vows is not enough to make him a Bhikkhu.

But he who is above both good and evil, who leads a pure life, who walks with understanding in this world, he can be called a Bhikkhu.

One who observes silence does not by that become a sage, if he is ignorant and foolish; but he who can weigh good and evil as in a balance and make his choice, him one can call a sage.

He who by contemplation measures this world and the other, he is a sage.

A man who does harm to living creatures does not become a Noble One. One who practises non-violence towards all creatures is called a Noble One.

It is neither by moral precepts and observances, nor by a wide knowledge, nor by practising meditation, nor by a solitary life, nor by thinking, "I have attained the bliss of liberation which is unknown to those who live in the world", that one can be called a Bhikkhu. Be on your guard, O Bhikkhus, until you have attained the extinction of all desire.

We shall take the last text. It is an interesting one.

"It is neither by moral precepts and observances, nor by a wide knowledge, nor by practising meditation, nor by a solitary life, nor by thinking", that one attains the true bliss; it is by getting rid of all desires. Certainly it is not easy to get rid of all desires, it sometimes needs a whole lifetime. But to tell the truth, it seems to be a very negative way, although at a certain stage of development, it is a discipline which it is very useful, even indispensable

87

to practise, if one does not want to deceive oneself. Because at first you begin by getting rid of the major desires, those that are most obvious and trouble you so much that you cannot even have any illusions about them; then come subtler desires that take the form of things that have to be done, that are necessary, even at times of commands from within, and it requires time and much sincerity to discover and overcome them; at last it seems as if you had done away with these wretched desires in the material world, in external things, in the world of feelings, in the emotions and sentiments, in the mental world as regards ideas, and then you find them again in the spiritual world, and there they are far more dangerous, more subtle, more penetrating and much more invisible and covered by such a saintly appearance that one dare not call them desires.

And when one has succeeded in overcoming all that, in discovering, dislodging and getting rid of them, even then one has done only the negative side of the work.

The Buddha said or has been made to say that when one is free from all desire, one necessarily enters into infinite bliss. This bliss may be a little dry and anyway it does not seem to me to be the quickest way.

If at the outset one were to seize the problem bodily, jump into it with courage and determination and, instead of undertaking a long, arduous, painful, disappointing hunt after desires, one gives oneself simply, totally, unconditionally, if one surrenders to the Supreme Reality, to the Supreme Will, to the Supreme Being, putting oneself entirely in His hands, in an upsurge of the whole being and all the elements of the being, without calculating, that would be the swiftest and the most radical way to get rid of the ego. People will say that it is difficult to do it, but at least a warmth is there, an ardour, an enthusiasm, a light, a beauty, an ardent and creative life.

It is true that without desire nothing much remains to sustain the ego and one has the impression that the consciousness becomes so hardened that if the ego crumbles into dust, then something of one's self also falls into dust and one is ready to enter into a Nirvana which is annihilation pure and simple.

But what we consider here as the true Nirvana is the disappearance of the ego into the splendour of the Supreme. And this way is what I call the positive way, the self-giving that is integral, total, perfect, without reserve, without bargaining.

In the mere fact of not thinking of oneself, not existing for oneself, referring nothing to oneself, thinking only of what is supremely beautiful, luminous, delightful, powerful, compassionate and infinite, there is such a profound delight that nothing can be compared to it.

This is the only thing that deserves... that is worthy of being attempted. All the rest is only marking time.

The difference is between climbing a mountain by going round and round, slowly, laboriously, step by step, for hundreds of years, and spreading invisible wings and soaring straight to the summit.

20 June 1958

The Path

The best of all paths is the Eightfold Path; the best of all truths is the Fourfold Truth; the best of all states is freedom from attachment; the best among men is the One who sees, the Buddha.

Truly, this is the Path; there is no other which leads to purification of vision. Follow this Path and Mara will be confounded.

By following this Path, you put an end to suffering. This Path I have made known, since I learned to remove the thorns (of life).

The effort must come from oneself. The Tathagatas only point out the Path. Those who meditate and tread this Path are delivered from the bondage of Mara.

"All conditioned things are impermanent." When one has seen that by realisation, he is delivered from sorrow. That is the Path of purity.

"All conditioned things are subject to suffering." When one has seen that by realisation, he is delivered from sorrow. That is the Path of purity.

"All things are insubstantial." When one has seen that by realisation, he is delivered from sorrow. That is the Path of purity.

He who though young and strong, does not act when it is time to act, is given to indolence, and his mind is full of vain thoughts; one who is so indolent will not find the Path of wisdom.

Moderation in speech, control of the mind, abstention from evil actions, thus these three modes of action are to be purified first of all, to attain the Path shown by the sages.

From meditation wisdom springs, without meditation wisdom declines. Knowing the two paths of progress and decline, a man should choose the Path which will increase his wisdom.

Cut down all the forest (of desires) and not one tree alone; for from this forest springs fear. Cut down this forest of trees and undergrowth, O Bhikkhus. Be free from desire.

As long as one has not rooted out of oneself entirely the desire of a man for a woman, the mind is captive, as dependent as a suckling on its mother.

Root out self-love, as one plucks with his hand an autumn lotus. Cherish only the Path of the peace of Nirvana that the Sugata[1] has taught us.

Here shall I live in the rainy season; I shall stay there in the winter and elsewhere in the summer. Thus thinks the fool and knows not what may befall him.

And this man who is attached to his children and his cattle, is seized by death and carried off, as a sleeping village is swept away by torrential floods.

Neither children, nor father, nor family can save us. When death seizes us, our kinsmen cannot save us.

---

[1] The Buddha.

Knowing this perfectly, the intelligent man, guided by good conduct, does not delay in taking up the path which leads to Nirvana.

Here are some very useful recommendations: moderation in speech, control of the mind, abstention from evil actions. This is very good.

Here is something radical, but it is also very good: "As long as one has not rooted out of oneself entirely the desire of a man for a woman, the mind is captive, as dependent as a suckling on its mother."

And finally: "Root out self-love, as one plucks with his hand an autumn lotus." These are good subjects for meditation.

These recommendations seem to have been meant for people who are just at the beginning of the Path from the intellectual point of view. We can easily imagine a gathering of country people, people with simple minds, to whom one has to say, "Listen carefully, it is no use making plans, for you do not know what will happen to you tomorrow. You are amassing wealth, you are taking your ease among your family, you are making schemes for tomorrow and for the day after, and you are not aware that death is on the watch and that at any moment it can fall on you."

All the same, there is a slightly more advanced stage of intellectual development in which these things need not be said — one must live them! Live in the consciousness that things are altogether impermanent, never become attached, if you are to be free to progress with the universe and grow according to the eternal rhythm. This one understands. But what is important is to practise it. Here one has the impression that these things were told to people who had never thought of them before and so they had the full power of an active force.

After all, in spite of all appearances, humanity progresses; it has progressed particularly in the mind. There are things that no longer need to be said.... Or else one must go to countries that are at a very primitive stage, and even so... ideas have spread everywhere, the mental light has spread everywhere and in the most unexpected places one finds instances of receptivity and understanding.

One really has the impression that during the last century a light came and spread upon the earth with the result that certain ideas, which were once idea-forces, new ideas with the power to stir up the consciousness in men, have lost their relevance, they are now old. A new light is at work.

In practice, the progress is not very great, even in some respects perhaps there has been a retrogression, but in the mind, in the understanding, in the intellectual vision of things, there has truly been a great change.

It seems we are marching on the way at an accelerated pace and these things which used to be of the first importance are becoming almost commonplace in the light of new discoveries. Life as it is is bad, disorder is everywhere, suffering is everywhere, confusion is everywhere, chaos is everywhere, ignorance is everywhere — we all know it, don't we? It seems so hackneyed.

But that one can emerge from it through a total realisation, a total transformation, through a new light that will establish order and harmony in things, is a message of hope that has to be given. This is the true, the dynamic message.

A new life must be built.

Then all these difficulties that seemed so unsurmountable — oh! they fall of themselves.

When you can live in light and joy, are you going to cling to shadow and suffering?

27 June 1958

93

Miscellany

If renouncing the slightest happiness enables him to re-alise a greater one, the intelligent man should renounce the lesser for the sake of the greater.

If he seeks his own happiness by harming others, bound by hate, he remains the slave of hatred.

To neglect what should be done and to do what should be neglected is to increase in arrogance and negligence.

To be constantly mindful of the true nature of the body, not to seek what is evil, to pursue with perseverance what is good, is to have right understanding; thus, all one's impurity disappears.

Having killed his father (ego), his mother (desire) and the two warrior kings (wrong views), having destroyed the kingdom (of the senses) and all its dependencies, the Brahmin lives free from evil.

Having killed father, mother, the two warrior kings and the tiger (mental hindrances), the Brahmin lives free from evil.

The disciples of Gautama are alert and truly awakened, for, day and night, their attention is turned to the Buddha, the Dhamma[1] and the Sangha.[2]

The disciples of Gautama are alert and truly awakened, for, day and night, their attention remains fixed on the Doctrine.

---

[1] The Law; the Teaching.
[2] The Community.

The disciples of Gautama are alert and truly awakened, for, day and night, their attention remains fixed on the Sangha.

The disciples of Gautama are alert and truly awakened, for, day and night, they remain aware of the true nature of the body.

The disciples of Gautama are alert and truly awakened, for, day and night, they delight in compassion.

The disciples of Gautama are alert and truly awakened, for, day and night, they take pleasure in meditation.

It is hard to renounce the world; it is equally hard to enjoy the world. Difficult and sorrowful is household life. It is painful to be with those who are not our equals and it is painful to wander in the cycle of births. Therefore, do not follow after sorrow nor be a wanderer without a goal.

The man who is full of faith and goodness, who possesses glory and wealth, is revered wherever he goes.

Men of goodness shine afar like the snowy peaks of the Himalayas. Whereas wicked men are no more visible than arrows shot in the night.

The man who eats alone, sleeps alone, walks alone untiring in his self-mastery, will delight in the solitary life of the forests.

Still you should not be mistaken. For I believe all these are images rather than material facts, because it is quite certain that eating alone, sleeping alone, living in the forest all alone is not enough to give you freedom of spirit.

It has been noticed that most people who live alone in the forest become friendly with all the animals and plants around them; but it is not at all the fact of being all alone that gives you the power of entering into an inner contemplation and living in communion with the Supreme Truth. Perhaps it is easier, when by force of circumstance you have nothing else to do, but I am not convinced of it. One can always invent occupations and it seems to me, according to my experience of life, that if one succeeds in subduing one's nature in the midst of difficulties, if one endeavours to be all alone within oneself with the eternal Presence, while keeping the same surroundings which the Grace has given us, the realisation which one obtains then is infinitely more true, more profound, more lasting.

To run away from difficulties in order to conquer them is not a solution. It is very attractive. In those who seek the spiritual life, there is something which says, "Oh! to sit down under a tree, all alone, to remain in meditation, not to have the temptation to speak or act, how fine it must be!" It is because there is a very strong formation in this direction, but it is very illusory.

The best meditations are those that one has all of a sudden, because they take possession of you as an imperative necessity. You have no choice but to concentrate, to meditate, to look beyond the appearances. And it is not necessarily in the solitude of the forest that it seizes you, it happens when something in you is ready, when the time has come, when the true need is there, when the Grace is with you.

It seems to me that humanity has made some progress and the true victory must be won in life itself.

You must know how to live alone with the Eternal and Infinite in the midst of all circumstances. You must know how to be free, with the Supreme as your companion, in the midst of all occupations. That is indeed the true victory.

14 July 1958

Niraya (Hell)

One who speaks untruth goes to Hell like one who, when he has done a thing, says: "I did not do it." Both, after death, will share the same fate, for these are men of evil.

Though they wear the yellow robe, those who are dissolute and evil-natured, their evil actions will cause them to be reborn in Hell.

It would be better to swallow a red-hot iron ball than to live on alms while leading a dissolute life.

Four punishments await the unscrupulous man who covets the wife of another: shame, troubled sleep, condemnation and Hell.

So he acquires an evil reputation and an evil birth; brief is the pleasure of the anxious pair, heavy the punishment of the law-giver. Let no man therefore seek the wife of another.

Just as Kusa grass cuts the hand if wrongly handled, so also asceticism wrongly understood leads to Niraya.

A duty carelessly fulfilled, a rule wrongly observed and a virtuous life followed out of fear, none of these will bring good results.

If a thing is to be done, do it with zeal. An ascetic with lax habits will stir up the dust (of the passions).

An evil deed is better left undone, for he who does it will be tormented by it. It is better to do a good deed, for he who does it will not have cause to repent it.

As a frontier city is well fortified both within and without, so one should guard oneself, so as not to waste a single moment of wakefulness; for those who lose this opportunity, even if only for a moment, will suffer indeed for it when in Hell.

Those who feel shame when there is no cause for shame, and those who feel no shame when there is cause to be ashamed, these deluded ones are destined to a painful state.

Those who are afraid of what should not be feared, and those who do not fear what is to be feared, these deluded ones are destined to a painful state.

Those who see evil where there is none, and those who do not see it where it is, these deluded ones are destined to a painful state.

Those who recognise evil to be evil, and good to be good, these who have right judgment are bound to enjoy happiness.

As in all these teachings there are always several ways of understanding them. The external way is quite commonplace. In all moral principles, the same thing is always said. This Niraya for example, which some take as a kind of hell where one is punished for one's sins, has also another sense. The true sense of Niraya is that particular kind of atmosphere which one creates around oneself when one acts in contradiction, not with outer moral rules or social principles, but with the inner law of one's being, the particular truth of each one which ought to govern all the movements of our consciousness and all the acts of our body. The inner law, the truth of the being is the divine Presence in every human being, which should be the master and guide of our life.

When you acquire the habit of listening to this inner law,

when you obey it, follow it, try more and more to let it guide your life, you create around you an atmosphere of truth and peace and harmony which naturally reacts upon circumstances and forms, so to say, the atmosphere in which you live. When you are a being of justice, truth, harmony, compassion, understanding, of perfect goodwill, this inner attitude, the more sincere and total it is, the more it reacts upon the external circumstances; not that it necessarily diminishes the difficulties of life, but it gives these difficulties a new meaning and that allows you to face them with a new strength and a new wisdom; whereas the man, the human being who follows his impulses, who obeys his desires, who has no time for scruples, who comes to live in complete cynicism, not caring for the effect that his life has upon others or for the more or less harmful consequences of his acts, creates for himself an atmosphere of ugliness, selfishness, conflict and bad will which necessarily acts more and more upon his consciousness and gives a bitterness to his life that in the end becomes a perpetual torment.

Of course this does not mean that such a man will not succeed in what he undertakes, that he will not be able to possess what he desires; these external advantages disappear only when there is within the inmost being a spark of sincerity which persists and makes him worthy of this misfortune.

If you see a bad man become unlucky and miserable, you must immediately respect him. It means that the flame of inner sincerity is not altogether extinguished and something still reacts to his bad actions.

Finally, that leads us again to the observation that you must never, never judge on appearances and that all the judgments you make from outward circumstances are always, necessarily false judgments.

To have a glimpse of the Truth, one must take at least one step back in one's consciousness, enter a little more deeply into one's being and try to perceive the play of forces behind the appearances and the divine Presence behind the play of forces.

25 July 1958

The Elephant

As the elephant on the battlefield endures the arrow shot from the bow, so also shall I patiently bear insult, for truly there are many of evil mind in the world.

It is a tamed elephant that is led to the battlefield; one whom the Raja rides. The best among men is he who patiently bears insult.

Trained mules are excellent, as also the thoroughbreds of Sindh and the mighty tuskers. Better yet is the man who has brought himself under control.

Not by mounting one of these animals does one attain the unexplored path, but by mastering oneself. By that mastery one attains it.

In the mating season it is difficult to control the mighty elephant Dhanapalako.[1] When he is chained he refuses to eat, he yearns only to be once more a wild elephant of the forest.

When a man is slothful and gluttonous, always sleepy and rolling from side to side like a fat hog in the mud — this fool is compelled to be born over and over again.

Once this mind wandered where it would from one thing to another, according to its pleasure, but now I shall master it completely as the mahout with his goad masters the elephant in rut.

---

[1] One who guards the treasure.

Delight in vigilance, guard carefully your mind. Lift yourself out of evil as the elephant sunk in a swamp.

If for company you find a prudent friend, who leads a good life, who is intelligent and self-controlled, overcoming all obstacles, do not hesitate to set out with him joyfully and courageously.

And if you do not meet with such a friend, who leads a good life, who is intelligent and self-controlled, then like a king renouncing a kingdom he has conquered, or like a solitary elephant in the forest follow your path alone.

It is better to live alone, for one cannot take a fool as a companion. It is better to live alone and do no evil, carefree, like the elephant in the jungle.

It is good to have friends when need arises. It is good to be satisfied with what one has. It is good, at the hour of death, to have acquired merit. It is good to leave all grief behind you.

In this world it is a joy to respect one's mother; it is a joy to respect one's father; it is a joy to honour the monks; it is a joy to revere the Brahmins.[2]

It is a joy to live purely throughout one's life. It is a joy to have a steadfast faith. It is a joy to acquire wisdom. It is a joy to abstain from all evil.

The first verse gives some very wise advice: the war elephant who has been well trained does not start running away as soon as he receives an arrow. He continues to advance and bears the pain, with no change in his attitude of heroic resistance. Those who wish

---

[2] The holy men; the men of wisdom.

to follow the true path will naturally be exposed to the attacks of all forms of bad will, which not only do not understand, but generally hate what they do not understand.

If you are worried, grieved or even discouraged by the malicious stupidities that men say about you, you will not advance far on the way. And such things come to you, not because you are unlucky or because your lot is not a happy one, but because, on the contrary, the divine Consciousness and the divine Grace take your resolution seriously and allow the circumstances to become a touchstone on your way, to see whether your resolution is sincere and whether you are strong enough to face the difficulties.

Therefore, if anyone sneers at you or says something that is not very charitable, the first thing you should do is to look within yourself for whatever weakness or imperfection has allowed such a thing to happen and not to be disconsolate, indignant or aggrieved, because people do not appreciate you at what you think to be your true value; on the contrary, you must be thankful to the divine Grace for having pointed out to you the weakness or imperfection or deformation that you must correct.

Therefore, instead of being unhappy, you can be fully satisfied and derive advantage, a great advantage from the harm that was intended against you.

Besides, if you truly want to follow the path and practise yoga, you must not do it for appreciation or honour, you must do it because it is an imperative need of your being, because you cannot be happy in any other way. Whether people appreciate you or do not appreciate you, it is of absolutely no importance. You may tell yourself beforehand that the further you are from ordinary men, foreign to the ordinary mode of being, the less people will appreciate you, quite naturally, because they will not understand you. And I repeat, it has absolutely no importance.

True sincerity consists in advancing on the way because you cannot do otherwise, to consecrate yourself to the divine life because you cannot do otherwise, to seek to transform your being and come out into the light because you cannot do otherwise, because it is the purpose of your life.

When it is like that you may be sure that you are on the right path.

1 August 1958

Craving

The craving of a heedless man grows like the Maluva creeper. Like a monkey seeking fruits in the forest, he leaps from life to life.

For one who in the world is overcome by the craving that clings, his miseries increase like Birana grass after the rains.

For one who in this world can overcome this craving that clings and is so difficult to master, his sorrows fall away like water from a lotus leaf.

To all who are gathered here, I say for your welfare: pull out the roots of your craving, as you uproot Birana grass. Do not let Mara crush you again and again as a flood crushes a reed.

As a tree, though felled, springs up once more if the roots remain intact, even so sorrow will return again and again until all craving is rooted out.

The misguided man, who cannot resist the thirty-six strong currents of craving, is swept away by the flood of his eagerness for pleasure.

Everywhere these currents flow and the creeper (of craving) springs up and increases. Wherever you see it springing up, cut out its roots with the force of wisdom.

Allowing their minds to be attracted by the enjoyment of transient objects, men who crave pleasure become a prey to birth and to decay.

Beset by craving, men run around like a hare in a trap. Bound by the chains of attachment, they come again and again to sorrow.

Beset by craving, men run around like a hare in a trap. Therefore, O Bhikkhu, desiring deliverance from passion, destroy your craving.

One who, delivered from craving, yet runs back to it, lo, he is like a freed man who returns to bondage.

What the wise call a strong bond is not made of iron, wood or rope; but the craving for jewels and ornaments, for wife and children, is a far stronger bond.

The wise say that it pulls you downward, and though it seems to be loose, it is hard to be rid of. This too the wise cut off; renouncing the pleasures of the senses, free from craving, they take to the homeless life.

Those who are bound by their passions are drawn back into the stream, like a spider caught in his own web. This too the wise cut off; renouncing the pleasures of the senses, free from craving, they take to the homeless life.

Be free from the past, be free from the future, be free from the present. Cross over to the other shore of existence; when the mind is wholly delivered, you shall come no more to birth and death.

One who is troubled by evil thoughts, who is controlled by his passions, who seeks only pleasure, his craving grows steadily; he makes his bonds strong indeed.

One who delights in subduing evil thoughts, who is vigilant and can distinguish impurities, he will put an end to his cravings, he shall break the bonds of Mara.

He who has reached the goal, who is without fear and free from craving and impurity, he has plucked out the thorns of existence; this is his last incarnation.

One who is free from craving, unattached, who knows the words and their meanings, who knows the arrangement of the texts in their sequence, he indeed has put on his last body. He alone is called "The Man of Great Wisdom."

I have vanquished all, I know all; unconditioned, all-renouncing, delivered by the extinction of craving, having understood all by myself, whom shall I call my teacher?

The gift of Truth excels all gifts; the savour of Truth excels all savours; delight in Truth excels all delights; deliverance from craving overcomes all suffering.

Riches ruin the fool, but not one who seeks the other shore. By craving for riches, the fool ruins himself and others with him.

Weeds are the bane of the fields; passion the bane of mankind. Therefore whatever is given to those freed from passions yields abundant fruit.

Weeds are the bane of the fields; hatred the bane of mankind. Therefore whatever is given to those freed from hatred yields abundant fruit.

Weeds are the bane of the fields; delusion the bane of mankind. Therefore whatever is given to those freed from delusion yields abundant fruit.

Weeds are the bane of the fields; desires the bane of mankind. Therefore whatever is given to those freed from desires yields abundant fruit.

We shall keep the last one to meditate on.

8 August 1958

The Bhikkhu

To control the eye is good; to control the ear is good; to control the nose and the tongue is good.

It is good to control one's actions, words, mind. Control in all things is good. The Bhikkhu who controls himself entirely is delivered from all suffering.

The man who is master over his hands, his feet and his tongue, who controls himself wholly, who delights in meditation, who is calm and leads a solitary life, can be called a Bhikkhu.

The Bhikkhu who is master over his tongue and is moderate in speech, who is modest, who luminously interprets the Doctrine, in truth his words are as sweet as honey.

The Bhikkhu who lives by the Doctrine, who delights in the Doctrine, who meditates on the Doctrine, who knows the Doctrine thoroughly, surely cannot fall away from the Doctrine.

The Bhikkhu should not treat his own progress (in wisdom and goodness) lightly, nor envy the progress of others; for the Bhikkhu who is envious cannot achieve concentration.

Even if the progress he has made is slight, the Bhikkhu should not despise it; if his life is pure and his effort persevering, the gods themselves shall praise him for it.

One who is not attached to name and form, who does not think, "This belongs to me", and who does not grieve over what does not exist, he, in truth, is called a Bhikkhu.

The Bhikkhu who lives a life of loving kindness and who is filled with faith in the teaching of the Enlightened One, that Bhikkhu will attain the peace of Nirvana, the supreme bliss from which every conditioned element has vanished.

Empty this boat, O Bhikkhu; once lightened, the boat of your body will sail more lightly and having rejected desire and hatred you shall enter Nirvana.

Break the five bonds (belief in the ego, doubt, belief in vain rites and ceremonies, craving and bad will). Renounce these five other bonds (the desire to live in the world of forms, the desire to live in the subtle world, pride, restlessness and ignorance). Cultivate these five (faith, energy, mindfulness, meditation, and wisdom). The Bhikkhu who is thus five times free is said to be "he who has crossed over the flood".

Meditate, O Bhikkhus, do not be negligent. Your minds should not turn towards the pleasures of the senses; for if by negligence you swallowed a red-hot iron ball, when you felt the burning you would lament, crying, "Oh, how painful it is!"

For one without knowledge there is no meditation; without meditation there is no knowledge. One in whom there is both meditation and knowledge is near to Nirvana.

The Bhikkhu who has entered the abode of emptiness, the Bhikkhu of serene mind, enjoys delight beyond the human, in the clear vision of the Doctrine.

Each time that he concentrates on the appearance and disappearance of all conditioned things, he enjoys the happiness and the delight of those who have attained immortality.

These things are for the wise Bhikkhu the very basis of the religious life: mastery of the senses, contentment, conduct according to the code of discipline, association with noble friends who lead a life of constant purity.

The Bhikkhu should be cordial, kind and polite; thus in the fullness of his joy, he will put an end to suffering.

Just as the jasmine sheds its faded petals, so also the Bhikkhu sheds desire and hatred.

Calm in action, calm in speech, calm in mind, serene, emptied of all earthly appetites, this Bhikkhu is called "The Serene One".

Let him arouse himself, let him examine himself; thus self-guarded and vigilant, the Bhikkhu will live in happiness.

In truth, one is one's own protector, one's own refuge. Know therefore how to control yourself as the horse-dealer controls a noble steed.

Filled with gladness and faith by the teaching of the Buddha, the Bhikkhu attains the state of perfect peace, cessation of all compounded existence.

The young Bhikkhu who consecrates himself to the Teaching of the Enlightened One, illumines this world like the moon coming forth from behind the clouds.

One piece of advice given here is that one should always be kind. It should not be mistaken for the sort of advice people normally give. It says something interesting, even very interesting. My comment is: Always be kind and you will be free from suffering, always be contented and happy, and you will radiate your quiet happiness.

It is particularly noticeable that all the digestive functions are extremely sensitive to an attitude that is critical, bitter, full of ill-will, to a sour judgment. Nothing disturbs the functioning of the digestion more than that. And it is a vicious circle: the more the digestive function is disturbed, the more unkind you become, critical, dissatisfied with life and things and people. So you can't find any way out. And there is only one cure: to deliberately drop this attitude, to absolutely forbid yourself to have it and to impose upon yourself, by constant self-control, a deliberate attitude of all-comprehending kindness. Just try and you will see that you feel much better.

22 August 1958

The Brahmin

Strive, O Brahmin! Seal up the current (of craving), cast away all pleasures of the senses. Knowing how to uproot the elements of existence you shall know the Uncreated.

When the Brahmin has attained the summit of the two paths (concentration and insight), all bonds fall away and he possesses the Knowledge.

One for whom neither the inner nor the outer exist, neither one nor the other, who is free from fear and bondage, him I consider to be a Brahmin.

One who is given to meditation and is freed of impurities, who is without stain, who has fulfilled his duty, who has attained the highest goal, him I consider to be a Brahmin.

By day the sun shines; by night the moon. In his armour the warrior shines; in meditation the Brahmin shines. Day and night, without ceasing, the Buddha is radiant.

The man who has rejected evil is a Brahmin. One whose behaviour is disciplined is a monk; an ascetic is one who is purged of impurities.

One should not strike a Brahmin, and the Brahmin should not strike back. Shame on one who strikes a Brahmin. Shame on the Brahmin who strikes back.

For a Brahmin there is nothing better than to restrain the mind from the pleasures of life. As he removes bad intentions, so he appeases his sufferings.

One who does no evil by act, word or thought, the man who is restrained in these three, him I consider to be a Brahmin.

Whosoever teaches you the Doctrine of the Perfectly Enlightened One, render him homage and venerate him as the Brahmin does the sacred fire.

Neither by matted hair, nor ancestry, nor by birth does one become a Brahmin. One in whom abide truth and righteousness, he is pure, he is a true Brahmin.

What value has your matted hair, O foolish man? What value has the antelope skin you wear? Within you lies a jungle of passions, you have only the appearance of purity.

The man dressed in cast-off robes, who is emaciated, whose veins stand out on his body, who meditates alone in the forest, him I consider to be a Brahmin.

But I do not call him a Brahmin, although he is of brahmin origin or born of a brahmin mother, he who is rich and arrogant. He who possesses nothing, who is attached to nothing, him I consider to be a Brahmin.

He who has broken all bonds, who no longer fears anything, who has overcome all ties, who is liberated, him I consider to be a Brahmin.

One who little by little has broken the thong (of mind) and the straps (of attachment), who has cut the chain (of doubt) with its links (of evil tendencies) and who has rejected the yoke (of ignorance), who is enlightened, him I consider to be a Brahmin.

113

He who is without resentment, who bears reproaches, blows and chains, whose patience is his true strength, him I consider to be a Brahmin.

He who is free from anger, who is faithful to his faith, good and without craving, who has mastered himself and taken a body for the last time, him I consider to be a Brahmin.

He who is no more attached to the pleasures of the senses than a drop of water to the lotus leaf, or a mustard seed to the point of a needle, him I consider to be a Brahmin.

He who, in this life, has realised the cessation of suffering, who has laid down the burden and has liberated himself (from the yoke of attachment), him I consider to be a Brahmin.

The intelligent man, gifted with profound wisdom, discerning the good and the evil path, who has attained the supreme goal, him I consider to be a Brahmin.

One who seeks the company neither of householders nor of monks, who has no home and few needs, him I consider to be a Brahmin.

One who does no harm to any creature, whether strong or weak, who does not kill nor cause to be killed, him I consider to be a Brahmin.

Friendly amid the unfriendly, calm amid the violent, unselfish amid the selfish, him I consider to be a Brahmin.

He from whom passion and hatred, pride and pretence have fallen away, as a mustard seed falls from the point of a needle, him I consider to be a Brahmin.

One who speaks only words that are sweet, instructive, true, and who offends no one, him I consider to be a Brahmin.

One who in this world takes nothing but what he is given, whether it be little or much, short or long, good or bad, him I consider to be a Brahmin.

One who has no more desires in this world or the other, who has no more craving, who is free, him I consider to be a Brahmin.

One in whom desire exists no more, one who has attained the perfection of knowledge, who has cast away all doubt and who has sounded the depths of immortality, him I consider to be a Brahmin.

One who in this world has broken all ties (of good and evil) and who is delivered from grief, from taints and impurities, him I consider to be a Brahmin.

One who, like the moon, is spotless, pure, clear, serene, from whom the thirst of earthly desires has vanished, him I consider to be a Brahmin.

One who has escaped from the cycle of births, this muddy path, this thorny road, and who has attained the other shore, is given to meditation, void of desire, free from doubt, detached from all things and at peace, him I consider to be a Brahmin.

One in whom all passion is destroyed and who, renouncing worldly pleasures, has left the household life and taken to the homeless life, him I consider to be a Brahmin.

115

He in whom all craving is dead and who, renouncing worldly pleasures, has left the household life, who has quenched the thirst of becoming, him I consider to be a Brahmin.

One who has rejected all earthly ties and has gone beyond all heavenly ties, who is delivered from all ties, him I consider to be a Brahmin.

One who has put aside liking and disliking, who is indifferent, who is freed from all attachment and all fetters, who has conquered all the worlds, this hero I consider to be a Brahmin.

He who possesses the perfect knowledge of the birth and death of all beings and who is freed from all ties, he is a Blessed One, an Awakened One, him I consider to be a Brahmin.

He whose future state is unknown to the gods, the demigods and mortals, who is without desire and without impurity, who has become an adept, him I consider to be a Brahmin.

He who no longer possesses anything, neither past nor present nor future, who owns nothing, who no longer clings to anything, that one I consider to be a Brahmin.

The Noble, the Excellent, the Hero, the great Sage, the Victor, the Impassive, the Pure, the Enlightened, him I consider to be a Brahmin.

One who knows his previous lives, one who perceives the heavens and the hells, who has come to the end of births, who has attained perfect vision, the Sage accomplished

116

in all accomplishments, him in truth I consider to be a Brahmin.

Such is the conclusion of the Dhammapada and if we have put into practice — to use its image — only a mustard seed of all that has been taught to us, well, we have not wasted our time.

There is one thing which is not spoken of here, in the Dhammapada: a supreme disinterestedness and a supreme liberation is to follow the discipline of self-perfection, the march of progress, not with a precise end in view as described here, the liberation of Nirvana, but because this march of progress is the profound law and the purpose of earthly life, the truth of universal existence and because you put yourself in harmony with it, spontaneously, whatever the result may be.

There is a deep trust in the divine Grace, a total surrender to the divine Will, an integral adhesion to the divine Plan which makes one do the thing to be done without concern for the result. That is the perfect liberation.

That is truly the abolition of suffering. The consciousness is filled with an unchanging delight and each step you take reveals a marvel of splendour.

We are grateful to the Buddha for what he has brought for human progress and, as I told you at the beginning, we shall try to realise a little of all the beautiful things he has taught us, but we shall leave the goal and the result of our endeavour to the Supreme Wisdom that surpasses all understanding.

5 September 1958

Other Titles
by The Mother

SEARCH FOR THE SOUL IN EVERDAY LIVING
by The Mother

Excellent introduction to the Mother's teachings, including chapters on "to be conscious", concentration and meditation, progress, obstacles, etc. *Search For The Soul* gives the seekers practical steps which can be taken HERE AND NOW. In addition, it points out the direction and the goal, clearly and in a language that everyone can grasp. The Mother's teachings touch the soul and reveal its nature with an immediacy and clarity which are undeniable.

ISBN 0-941524-57-4   162pp pb $8.95

THE SOUL AND ITS POWERS
by The Mother

Man has been searching for the meaning of life even from before the birth of Christ. Various religious/spiritual disciplines have developed over the centuries. But inevitably the solution was to escape from life towards a nirvana or a heaven that gave peace and salvation but left this earth unchanged. The Mother and Sri Aurobindo had a contrary view however, formulated upon their experiences and realizations. There is more to life than to escape from it.

ISBN 0-941524-67-1   147pp pb $9.95

FLOWERS AND THEIR MESSAGES, US EDITION
by The Mother

By entering into contact with the nature of a flower, its inner truth...one knows what it represents...if you are in contact with it, if you feel it, you can get an impression which may be translated as a thought. There is a kind of identification with the vibration, a perception of the quality that it represents...little by little there occurs a close approach between these vibrations, that are of the vital-emotional order, and the vibration of mental thought.

ISBN 0-941524-68-X 309pp pb $29.95

Available from your local bookseller or
Lotus Press, PO Box 325, Twin Lakes, WI 53181 • 262-889-8561
www.lotuspress.com • email: lotuspress@lotuspress.com